THROUGH HARSH WINTERS

THROUGH HARSH WINTERS

The Life of a Japanese Immigrant Woman

AKEMI KIKUMURA

Chandler & Sharp Publishers, Inc.

Novato, California

Library of Congress Cataloging in Publication Data

Tanaka, Michiko, 1904–
    Through harsh winters.

    (Chandler & Sharp publications in
anthropology and related fields)
    Bibliography: p.
    I. Tanaka, Michiko, 1904–   2. Japanese
Americans — California — Liberty — Biography.
3. Liberty (Calif.) — Biography.   I. Kikumura,
Akemi, 1944–   II. Title.   III. Series.
F869.L5T366   979.4'93   81–15534
ISBN 0-88316-544-9   AACR2
ISBN 0-88316-543-0 (pbk.)

*Chandler and Sharp recommends that librarians use the following
suggested alternative cataloging, which differs from that of the
Library of Congress in the details distinguished by* **boldface** *type:*

Kikumura, Akemi, 1944–
    Through harsh winters.

    (Chandler & Sharp publications in
anthropology and related fields)
    Bibliography: p.
    1. **Kikumura, Akemi, 1944–**   2. Japanese
Americans — California — Liberty — Biography.
3. Liberty (Calif.) — Biography.   I. **"Tanaka, Michiko"
(pseudonym), 1904–**   II. Title.   III. Series.
F869.L5T366   979.4'93   81–15534
ISBN 0-88316-544-9   AACR2
ISBN 0-88316-543-0 (pbk.)

International Standard Book Number:
      0-88316-544-9 (casebound edition)
      0-88316-543-0 (paperback edition)
Library of Congress Catalog Card Number: 81–15534
Printed in the United States of America.

Editor: W. L. Parker
Book designed by Joseph M. Roter.
Cover art and design for both editions by Qris Yamashita.
Composition by Publications Services of Marin.

SEVENTH PRINTING, 1989

*To My Family
in Japan and in America
and especially to
My Mother
and My Daughter Remi*

KU AREBA
RAKU ARI

Through harsh winters
Follow springs
— A Japanese Proverb

Contents

Preface

Great adventure in a land of promise was an image many young Japanese women had conjured up in their minds when they followed their men to America at the turn of the twentieth century. Innocent dreams were quickly shattered by the harsh realities of their everyday existence, for before long they found themselves engaged in hard physical labor in addition to taking care of children and tending to household chores.

The process of acculturating to American social and cultural life was particularly slow for the Issei (first-generation immigrant from Japan) women. Efforts at orienting themselves to their new environment were hindered by the inability to speak English, by confinement to home and children, by lack of relatives or any network of social organizations and friends, and by the barriers of racism and discrimination.

This book was written out of respect and admiration for these courageous women who had managed to transform hardship, suffering, and despair into determination, understanding, and hope. In an attempt to capture their spirit and to learn more about my own cultural heritage, I had decided to write a life history of my mother, using her own words (as I translated them) to tell a story about an Issei woman's experience in America.

The book is basically divided into three parts. The first part gives the reader a background into the research, describing the trip to Japan to find out more information about my mother's past. The second section contains the life history itself; this is the main body of the book. In the process of translating my mother's account, I have tried to remain as faithful as possible to her actual words in order to convey to the reader the flavor of her speech and to capture a better understanding of the individual. The names of people and some geographic locations have been changed, but all other information remains factual. The third part deals with reflections on my mother's past after the completion of the life history.

I have included two appendices: one on the Japanese American family and another on methodology. The first provides a brief overview of the Japanese family system before World War II and the social structure in which the Issei were reared; from this the reader can understand some of the continuities and discontinuities from Japan to America. In addition, this appendix looks at some aspects of culture change and persistence within the present Japanese American family. The appendix on methodology deals with the methods and procedures involved in the research process.

A.K.

June 1981

Acknowledgments

The completion of this book could not have been accomplished without the combined efforts of many people who were involved at various stages of its development; to them I wish to express my deep appreciation and gratitude.

The person most responsible for the completion of my study was Professor Hiroshi Wagatsuma, who played the role of both *sensei* and parent, mentor and friend, providing intellectual stimuli and emotional support. The conscientious dedication of his time, wisdom, and concern were priceless ingredients that I could not have managed without, for they sustained me through all phases of the preparation of this book. The interest and involvement of the Wagatsuma family, Oku-sama (Reiko), Erika, and Yuria, helped me to persevere in my research: to the entire Wagatsuma family, I wish to express my heartfelt thanks.

I also owe a great debt to Professor Lewis L. Langness, who commented upon the manuscript at various stages of its development. He provided inspiration and enjoyment through his brilliant intellect and good sense of humor which made my work possible. I will always remain grateful for his support.

A number of friends and scholars generously shared their time, knowledge, and interest. I want to especially thank Professor Harry H. L. Kitano, Professor Alexander Saxton, Professor John G. Kennedy, and Professor Pete Z. Snyder.

This book could not have been completed without the financial, technical, and administrative support of the following: The National

Institute of Mental Health (NIMH) for their graduate traineeship program, the Institute of American Cultures (IAC) for their research grant, the Asian American Studies Center at the University of California, Los Angeles, for their administration of the IAC grant, and Lupe Montano for typing the final manuscript.

The kindness, hospitality, and love that I received from my family in Japan are memories that will forever bring me warmth and joy. To my uncles, aunts, cousins, and their families, I owe one of the most thrilling and moving experiences of my life.

To my family in America, I owe a lifelong debt: to my sisters for their compassion, strength, and courage, to my brother for carrying the heavy burden of being the only son, and to my father for his hopes and dreams. To my husband, Gary Yano, I owe a special thanks for his unflagging support and encouragement.

Many hours were spent away from home doing field research, and I want to thank my daughter, Remi S. Manning, for her patience and understanding, and for teaching me more about life than all the books I read throughout my studies.

Finally, to my mother — "thanks" is not enough — I owe my life. The appreciation, respect, admiration, and love I hold for her is "deeper than the oceans and higher than the mountains." She has taught me through example that the strength, courage, understanding, and love of a parent and of a woman are infinite.

THROUGH HARSH WINTERS

FAMILY GENEALOGY

(Eldest to youngest siblings listed from left to right)

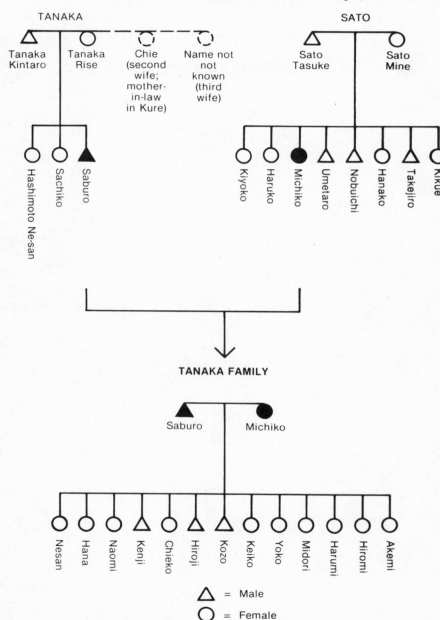

TANAKA

Tanaka Kintaro
Tanaka Rise
Chie (second wife; mother-in-law in Kure)
Name not not known (third wife)

Hashimoto Ne-san
Sachiko
Saburo

SATO

Sato Tasuke
Sato Mine

Kiyoko
Haruko
Michiko
Umetaro
Nobuichi
Hanako
Takejiro
Kikue

TANAKA FAMILY

Saburo
Michiko

Nesan
Hana
Naomi
Kenji
Chieko
Hiroji
Kozo
Keiko
Yoko
Midori
Harumi
Hiromi
Akemi

△ = Male

○ = Female

Introducing
My Mother's Family

My mother and father were born in Hiroshima, Japan, and came to America on a short trip with the intention of staying for just a few months. My father found a job as a farm laborer and my mother as a cook. But since their dreams of "success" did not fully mature, they were to remain in America never to return home again.

As a child I remember intently listening to my sisters talk about the family. I was never included in any of the discussions because I was the youngest, and knowing that with the slightest disturbance they would chase me out of the room, I quietly sat in the most inconspicuous spot of the room and listened. When the voices turned to murmurs, I was quickly whisked out the door. I always wondered what was being said behind those closed doors. I couldn't wait until I too would be included as part of that inner circle.

It was 22 years later that many of those "forbidden" stories would be revealed to me. I had decided to write a life history of my family focusing particularly on my mother. What was her life like before coming to America? Why did she leave her homeland? Life in America was not like anything she had imagined. How did she manage to survive the extraordinary hardships? Why didn't she return home? These were questions that always puzzled me.

The idea of going to Japan to see her family had not occurred to me at that time. Relatives in Japan? They were just imaginary figures to my older sisters and nonexistent to the younger ones, for the longer my parents stayed in America, the fewer were the stories about their families and dimmer their hopes of returning home: My father died without ever seeing his homeland again, and my mother was resigned to do the same.

In the fall of 1976 I was determined to make the trip that my parents never took. I urged my mother to get back in touch with her family. At first she hesitated, but with the persistent urging of both myself and other family members, she wrote her first letter home.

We nervously awaited a reply. Several weeks passed before a letter arrived from my mother's eldest sister, Haruko. I rushed to my mother's house to read my auntie's letter. Was she happy to hear from Mama or was it just a perfunctory, courtesy reply? To our relief, the letter conveyed a genuine warmth and enthusiasm. It had been the first time since the War that she had heard from Mama, and from that letter, regular correspondence between Mama and her sister began.

By February of 1977, plans for the trip were prudently outlined. With great care in choosing the proper words, Mama sent two letters: one to her eldest sister, Haruko, with whom she had been corresponding, and another to her eldest brother (four years younger than Mama), explaining that I was going to Japan to discover the family's history. Mama insisted that she must ask her eldest brother, Umetaro, to accommodate me because according to Japanese custom, it was his responsibility as head of the household. "Besides," Mama said, "he would be the one most financially capable since he inherited my parents' business."

Again we waited for a reply. Japanese relatives couldn't say no, but would they couch their negative response in politeness? And even if they consented, what kind of reception would I receive? Would they treat me like family? Or would I be rebuffed? Would I be able to gain the intimacy and trust I needed to uncover the sensitive information that I planned to gather? Mama kept repeating to me, "When I was a young girl in Japan my parents had a large business . . . wholesale sugar . . . now Ume-san has it. I'm sure they are still doing well and could accommodate you." But her repeated efforts to convince me (and perhaps herself) only filled me with more doubt.

About 15 years ago one of my sister's in-laws went to Hiroshima and dropped in to see my mother's family. They returned saying, "Umetaro-san was too busy counting his money; he barely lifted his head to say hello." Would they treat me the same way? Why shouldn't they? After all, Mama never kept in touch with them. She left Japan when she was nineteen and her brothers and sisters were still very young. What ties would remain even between brothers and sisters after 55 years of just a few letters and an occasional picture?

I'm sure this underlying fear of rejection was also running through my mother's mind. But she kept reassuring me that the Sato family was still prosperous and would welcome me. "You go back to Japan and see for yourself," she said. "Mama comes from a good family . . . a family that never suffered for money. You go back and see."

Mama had said that before but since Papa always belittled her, we sisters questioned whether Mama really was from the kind of family she described. How could a woman so poor and shabbily dressed be from such a good family? Why would they permit her to marry a man like Papa and come to America? Didn't people from "good" homes not allow their daughters to go to America and struggle as laborers?

The letter arrived at two o'clock in the morning: Special Delivery. It was from Itsue, Umetaro's wife. She gave Mama all the numbers where I could reach them. Her eldest son, Shōsō, was to meet me at the airport. They were waiting for me. I was on my way to Japan, to a very important mission.

It had been 55 years since Mama and Papa left Japan. They had sold Mama's kimonos, borrowed $150 from her parents and $350 from the Tanaka household, then boarded the *Korea Maru* along with 3000 others bound for San Francisco. I would repay Mama's debts and see for myself the place of her childhood. "I am *oya fukō* [undutiful to one's parents]," she said. "Please go to my father's grave and tell him Mama couldn't come. Tell him why I couldn't return all those years. Tell him at least that."

Mama claimed she was too old to return home now. Her excuse was, "I have a weak bladder. It's damaged from all the hard work I have done. That's why I hate to travel . . . it's like suffering." As she continued to tell me how much of a burden she would be if she were to accompany me, I thought of the main reason why she never went home before. It was the same reason why many Issei (first generation of Japanese who immigrated from their homeland) never returned. It was from shame — shame of returning to their homeland as someone who didn't succeed.

Mama would say, "How could I have gone back and raised my head knowing the abject life we were living in America? I never forgot that I did not repay the money we borrowed. From embarrassment I never went back."

Mama's guilt for not repaying her debts lay deep and when I told her that I planned to go to Takata to track down Papa's family, she pleaded with me, "Please don't say you'll look them up. I can't show my face to them. And believe me, they won't be happy to see you! There'll be nothing but trouble. Besides, you couldn't have enough money to go back and see them."

I pressed harder, "Why, Mama?" But she pursed her lips tightly and refused to give me any additional information. "Just let things be," she insisted, then changed the subject.

The eve of my departure I called my brother. When I told him I was going to Japan to see our relatives, he laughed and said, "Well, Dad's family won't be too glad to see you." I asked him why Mama had been so persistent about not visiting Papa's family and he proceeded to tell me why. (After my return from Japan, Mama related the same story to me herself.)

"You see, Dad was three years old when his father left for America and it wasn't until he was nineteen that he saw him again in San Francisco. Dad met Grandfather in San Francisco and they had to ask each other who they were. From there they went to Liberty where Grandfather had been farming.

"Dad and Grandfather bought some crops — 50 acres of peaches and 50 acres of grapes, and they combined their money together to make a profit. They made about $32,000 cash, which in those days was equivalent to a quarter or a half million dollars today. Then Grandfather said, 'You're young yet so you make your own money,' and he went back to Japan and bought some land. Dad was so angry that he refused to go to San Francisco to see his father off because he didn't even leave Dad with decent clothes to wear. But this man called Yamada said, 'It's your father, so go and see him off. Japan is 7000 miles away and you'll probably never see him again to the day he dies,' so Dad went, borrowing a horse and buggy, money and suit from Yamada. Since then Dad became a gambler.

"When Grandfather got older, he wrote a letter to Dad. You see, he had gotten remarried to another woman and had two or three kids by her. He said that since they were going to look after him until he died, he would give them the major part of his property, but he would set aside a small portion for Dad. Dad had intentions to send us back to Japan but it never happened."

So that's why they wouldn't be glad to see me! They would think that I had come back to claim the family fortune. Before World War II primogeniture was the law in Japan. My father was the only son; legally I would not have any rights to the property, but morally I would — at least my arrival would breed a lot of suspicion.

By the time my flight reached Japan I was nervous, full of anxiety, and exhausted from working out in my mind all the things that could possibly go wrong on my trip. I boarded a waiting bus like everyone else who was on the same flight, then quickly got off when I realized my baggage was still at the terminal where I landed. The bus left and I stood waiting, looking into everyone's eyes for some sign of recognition.

Nobody approached me. All kinds of thoughts swirled through my mind. Maybe they didn't come out to meet me and had expected me to catch a cab. The letter to Mama had said that since Hiroshima Airport was being remodeled, Shōsō, the eldest son of my mother's eldest brother Umetaro, would come after me at Iwakuni Airport, where I now waited. I called the numbers I had and finally reached a woman who told me to meet Shōsō at the Kinsey Hotel since only arriving and departing passengers were allowed on the airport premises, which was a military base. Shōsō would be waiting for me there at the hotel.

I quickly hailed a cab and the driver went into the hotel lobby to page Sato Shōsō from Hiroshima. Out from the lobby walked my cousin, a stocky man about forty, with short legs, broad shoulders and a barrel chest. He wore a brown suit with tapered trousers which he kept pulling up by the belt. His face was that of a self-assured man — confident, good-natured, healthy, with a ruddy complexion and gold teeth that he displayed with his generous smile.

He picked up my luggage and started to walk briskly away from the hotel to the train station. He told me that Mama's oldest sister Haruko and her youngest brother Takejiro were waiting to greet me at the Hiroshima station. With my luggage laden with brandy, books, tablets, tapes, and camera, we walked up and down many stairs before coming to our train stop. His strength surprised me as he easily lifted my luggage above the train seat.

When we arrived at Hiroshima station I became very anxious. What do I say? Shōsō looked around for his car, spotted it, then quickly walked in that direction. The man waiting inside jumped out to open the trunk and greeted me. It was Shōsō's younger brother Masahiro. We waited in the car for Auntie Haruko and Uncle Takejiro, who were somewhere in the station still waiting for my train, then left without them, knowing that they would catch up to us in Tomita where Uncle Umetaro and his wife Itsue awaited my arrival. They were to be my parents, my guardians, and Tomita would be my new home — the place I would stay for most of my trip.

We drove out of Hiroshima city and into the nearby mountainside. Tomita was about a half hour outside of Hiroshima where Shōsō had built a resort home for his mother and father, away from the hustle and bustle of the city. "Here my parents will live longer," Shōsō said. Our car climbed the mountain up narrow streets made for one car, passed many rice fields, and pulled into a driveway in front of a modern western-style suburban house.

Auntie Itsue, a delicately thin, attractive woman, stood at the door to greet me. I was expecting to see a distorted, scarred face because Shōsō had told me that the whole side of his mother's body and face were burned by the *pica* (atomic bomb). Through her high-pitched gentle voice I could hear the genuine feeling of welcome as I took my shoes off at the entrance.

When I entered the house I was taken aback by its elegance. The wooden floors glistened with polish. Carefully planned flower arrangements were placed in separate parts of the room against a backdrop of natural wood paneling. Uncle Umetaro sat on the couch in the living room and when he greeted me, I knew everything would be all right. Uncle broke into a broad smile. He looked so much like Mama that the close resemblance comforted me. My attention was drawn to his large eyes and full lips. His stature seemed even taller as he stood erect wearing a blue kimono.

Uncle studied me carefully as I began to talk. He wanted to know why I had come. He already knew but now he wanted to hear me say it. I told him that I planned to write a life history of my family, looking at the cultural changes from Japan to America. I wanted to know more about the Sato family, about my father's family, the place of their birth, their childhood, their reasons for emigrating to America.

Masahiro arrived at the house with his thirteen-year-old daughter Atsue. He sat quietly as his elder brother Shōsō took charge of the conversation when Uncle Umetaro wasn't talking. But it was definitely Uncle who was in charge of everything. As I spoke, they would all laugh at my Japanese. It was strange to them, I'm sure — a mixture of Hiroshima and Tokyo dialect, laced with childhood language.

Auntie Haruko and Uncle Takejiro finally arrived at 3:00 p.m. They were waiting for me at the wrong place and got lost again while trying to find the house. I was eager to meet my Auntie Haruko for Mama felt the closest to her. She was a small lady — much slighter than Mama. She wore her hair drawn back tightly into a bun, which emphasized her thin face and pointed chin. Her diamond-shaped eyes sloped downward and at the tip of her well-shaped nose rested a wart. I wondered how long she had that at the tip of her nose for in the picture that Mama had of her sister, she was a strikingly beautiful woman with a flawless complexion. Uncle Takejiro, the youngest of my mother's family (63 years old), looked older than Umetaro who was 70. He too was thin, as were all of Mama's brothers and sisters. His hands shook constantly as he drew the cup of coffee closer to his lips.

Auntie Haruko sat on the couch closest to me and as she began to talk the tears streamed from her eyes. She wanted to hear about Mama and while I told her about the hard life Mama had led in America, and about how Mama wanted to come home, and how she wanted to return the money they had borrowed from the Sato family, her tears flowed even more profusely. *"Michiko-san wa kuro shita kara neh* [My how she suffered],"* she kept repeating, and they all agreed how good it would have been if Mama had returned with me.

We sat down to dine. I got to sit between Uncle Umetaro and Auntie Haruko. *"Nan demo nai mono kedo* [it's nothing but . . .],"* they said but it was a beautiful spread: an exotic variety of rice cakes (topped with octopus, squid, abalone, shrimp, fish of all kinds) in a huge lacquered tray, chicken, sweet beans, lima beans, hard-boiled eggs, sliced tomatoes, cucumbers, and fresh apples and strawberries. The beer kept pouring along with the brandy. Shōsō and Uncle Umetaro savored each sip of the Napoleon brandy. It was the best gift that I could have brought from America.

With my Auntie Haruko's urging, I sang a few Japanese songs that Papa had taught me. My face flushed from the alcohol and I could feel my body finally starting to relax. Uncle Umetaro tapped me on the shoulder and asked me to turn on my tape recorder. He was going to sing a song for Mama. I was amazed. He sang like a professional with his large lips shaping into perfect configurations, and each note exploding on a consonant and carried forth on a vowel. His rhythm, tone, and quality were superb, but most of all, each song was delivered from the heart.

The conversations grew louder as the drinks continued to flow. Auntie Itsue pulled out a picture of herself and Uncle when they were learning Japanese dances. Light-hearted bantering filled the room and I sat back absorbing the good feeling. How fortunate is my mother's family. I never saw Mama sing or dance. She never had time to do flower arrangements or the tea ceremony or Japanese dances, although I knew she had learned to do all those things when she was a young girl.

The next morning I awoke at five o'clock. Tears welled in my eyes as I gazed at the glowing lantern in the garden. I cried for self-pity

— pity that we were deprived all our lives of the warmth and protection of a grandfather and grandmother, of uncles and aunts. But I cried especially for Mama . . . all the love and security she had missed. As I spent the evening with her brothers and sisters, I could just imagine Mama among them talking, gleaming with pride, love, companionship — all the things that she was deprived of when she left for America with a strange man. How lonely she must have been!

When I finally opened the sliding screen doors of my room, it was quite late. Auntie and Uncle had already eaten breakfast. Uncle kept urging me to take a bath. I wanted to wash my hair so I asked permission to do so in the bath. Auntie followed after me wearing a broad grin as she kindly said, "I will teach you the Japanese way. In Japan we don't drain the water after taking a bath. We wash ourselves outside the tub before getting in. We get the towel like this [she held either end of the towel and slid it back and forth across her back] and wash. Then never put the towel in the clean water. Using this pan, you scoop out the water and wash with it — wash your buttocks and everything. See? So the water is clean because you never scrub in the tub. You are clean before you get in the tub. The bath is just for soaking . . . it's only the three of us so it's clean. Then at the end of the day, we drain it." We both laughed. How stupid of me. Yesterday Uncle went in to take a bath, got undressed, and found the bath water all gone. I had drained it after getting out.

Auntie was busy making breakfast when I got out. After breakfast I invited her into my room to help me with the gifts I had brought from America. I told her, "Since you know all the relatives you can give me the best advice — please tell me what's best for whom." All the things that Mama and my sisters gave to me lay in front of us: the silver rings, the Kennedy coins, sheets, pens, Mexican blouses and shirts, a Jamaican dashiki, belt buckles, perfume, brandy, and an assortment of American-made items.

I could tell from the pleased look on Auntie's face that it was a wise move on my part to consult her. The UCLA T-shirt was the first item she spotted, "Aah, my grandson would really like this because he's an *oshare* [dandy], always primping." Then she carefully examined the rings, finally settling on one which she turned over and over, admiring the bold relief carved on the band.

"Please, Auntie, I want you to have it because this is the one that Mama likes too . . . when you look at it, you will think of her." Slipping the ring on her finger, she stretched her arms out to admire it from a distance. She let out a girlish giggle, "My, I have never worn anything as fancy. Tell your mother I will wear it and think of her."

By the time we straightened everything out, Auntie had decided that the UCLA T-Shirt and belt buckle would go to her grandsons. Her son Masahiro is *hade na* [fond of show] so he would enjoy the dashiki; her daughter-in-law and her granddaughter would really enjoy the Mexican blouses, and Shōsō would play golf with the Mexican shirt. "I can just see him on the golf course with the Mexican shirt and the silver bracelet," she giggled. "They would think *hade na!* [how fancy]! Everyone would look at him." Uncle sat in the living room listening to the transactions. Every now and then I could hear him chuckling, "You claimed everything for your own sons and grandchildren."

Auntie sat quietly now watching me while I sorted the gifts and put them neatly to one side of the room. Then with the same gentle tone of voice she had used to tell me about the bath, she said, "Don't tell anybody that you were married and that you're leaving a child back in America. You could tell me and Uncle but don't tell the others, especially the younger ones . . . you will smash their dreams. When they heard you were coming from America, they were all excited thinking that you would be about the same age. We tried to figure out how old you were by Michiko-san's age but in the picture you look like you're about 22." In the other room I could hear Uncle making sounds of disapproval. "You don't have to say such things to her," he told Auntie. But I reassured her that I had no intentions of telling anyone else, and after all was settled, we sat together in front of the window looking out over the garden. Auntie was so enthusiastic about helping me. Patiently she ran down the Sato genealogy, telling me the ages and bits of information about each family member.

That day Shōsō volunteered to take me to my grandparents' grave before the rains came. Uncle and Auntie picked flowers for the grave and vegetables for the main house in Machida. Their garden was incredible — planted in such a way as to form beautiful patterns of color and texture with the variety of vegetables. Shōsō arrived promptly at five, the height of the rush hour. When we reached the grave site, he casually filled a bucket with water to wash down the grave. I walked briskly behind trying to keep up with his pace.

The grave was just as grand as Mama said it would be. It was the most elegant one in the cemetery, standing over six feet tall and occupying the space of two plots. In the grave were the bones of Sato Grandfather and Grandmother and of Kiyoko, my mother's oldest sister who had died of stomach cancer. As Auntie lit the incense, I knelt and prayed. I told my grandparents that I had finally come home for Mama. As tears flowed for all those years Mama couldn't come back, I asked them for their forgiveness.

Auntie and Shōsō looked on proudly. Auntie spoke softly as she knelt down beside me, "With this your mother will have peace of mind. Your Mama would be proud of the grave. Tell Mama, *neh* . . . that Ume-san as head of the Sato family has used the Sato fortune wisely and has honored his ancestors. He has made sure to build a fine grave."

"Your Mama still sends money back each year so that on the night of August 14 we can set up a lantern on her behalf," said Shōsō in his loud voice, interrupting the communion that we had established. "Everyone can see that someone from America is honoring the grave because it is written: Tanaka Michiko of America."

From that day on, I began to call Shōsō *Onī-san* (big brother). It brought us closer together. Some times he would slip and call himself *Oji-san* (uncle), then correct himself again. He was pleased that I called him *Onī-san* for it made him feel younger. Onī-san was invaluable. He was my right-hand man. He would drive me every-where, set up my appointments, make the appropriate phone calls, help collect the genealogies, process the film, repair my tape recorder. I was truly indebted to him.

The next day I would go to the main house in Machida. This was the place where my mother grew up. Onī-san, his wife, and their two sons lived there now above the store. Up to a year ago Auntie and Uncle lived in Machida but as Uncle's health weakened, he sought permanent refuge in Tomita, leaving complete control of the business to Oni-san. It was there that I would discover my mother's past and hear the stories that she had told me come to life. The following life history is based on these memories she chose to tell me about her past.

The Life History

1

CHILDHOOD
(1904–1922)

The following history is my mother's, the memories she chose to tell me about her past life. The interviews were tape recorded in Japanese; I have translated it and made a few rearrangements to bring disconnected anecdotes together. But the story is my mother's.

I didn't know you had to suffer before you could understand life. When I was a young girl in Japan, suffering was unknown to me until I was eighteen. I never worried about making money. All my thoughts centered around play.

My family owned a confectionery and wholesale sugar store in Hiroshima City. I guess I was punished in my later life since I used to look down on our workers because they were poor. I'll never forget this one young man who worked for us. He told me I had the face of a poor person and that one day I would experience poverty. He said I did not understand anything about life, and he wrote me a note that I always remembered: *"Watashi no kōfuku wa mazushii ie ni aru* [My happiness is in a poor house]."

My parents never disciplined us; they were both busy with business. That's how it was with business people — they thought all they had to do with children was send them to school. From morning until night they would think about making money. People who got a salary were more concerned with disciplining their children than business people, who were more interested in enhancing profits.

My mother was a sharp, shrewd business woman. She made the Sato fortune. Not a bit of education — she couldn't even read or write but she was a genius. She didn't have to use an abacus. She could figure it all up in her head. Wearing black trousers and smoking a long, brown cigarette, Mama ordered everyone around. She was definitely the boss. Businessmen from all around would come to consult with her about their investments. She bought the neighboring stores: the confectionery shop, the blacksmith's, the noodle shop, and a tea shop.

My father was small because mother was so strong. He was afraid of her. "How much should I buy? How much should I sell it for?" he would ask. My Papa was like a *hotoke* [Buddha]. He never cheated anyone and even if he lost money, he never complained. He was the only one among his brothers who was successful and he shared his good fortune liberally. If his eldest brother went bankrupt, Papa would bankroll him; if his younger brother wanted to open a shop, he would lend him the capital only to find him vacationing in the country. He cried a lot over them.

Papa was a frugal man when it came to himself — never drank or smoked, never spent money to eat out. He would have a lunch made for him as he went to the countryside to collect money from his customers. He delivered sugar to them and collected the money after they sold it. Before, that's how it was: You didn't collect until the merchants sold your products.

During the winter we had twelve people helping in the store. We sold various kinds of sugar, beans, honey, flour, and made *yokan* [sweet jelly of beans], and grape and strawberry syrup. We would sell these syrups as far away as Shimonoseki, well beyond Hiroshima city. We advertised that it was healthy for your body because it didn't contain alcohol.

My mother . . . what a *yarite* [a person of ability]! She learned how to make these syrups in Osaka. Her eldest sister lived in Osaka and made syrup so she took the recipe and learned how to make it herself. Our young workers would try to steal the recipe from her but she guarded it with a careful eye. We manufactured the syrup in the back of our workshop, which had a lot of space. Our place was huge. It was always stocked full with rice that people brought to us.

Once there was a fire. We would put the *korizato* [sugar crystals] in vats but the sugar caught on fire and the flames rose above the roof of the workshop. The workers managed to contain the fire but we were terrified that the flames would leap out of control with the wind. In Japan they say that good fortune will not grace your doorstep for seven generations if your house was the place where a fire originated. Fire was more frightening than a thief because a village could disappear in one breath since all the buildings were made of wood and paper.

My Papa's youngest sister lived with us. She would get married and keep returning home. The marriages never lasted too long. With the last one she decided never to marry again and she came to live with us. She boiled the rice, made the dinners, and did all the household chores. I would work in the store after school but my mother didn't let me help too often because I gave everything to the customers. It is my nature to be giving. Papa would get mad at me and send me off to Iwakuni and Kuba to collect money from our customers. Since I was young, people gave me extra orders. I went as far as Shimonoseki.

I fought with my sisters and brothers over small matters. But when there are many relatives you do not get along. There were eight of us: three younger brothers and four sisters. I was third from the eldest. I was closest to Haruko, the sister right above me.

Summers I would go with my girlfriends to swim in the river and catch locusts. We often went to Tenji mountain to collect bracken, but the climb was the joy of it: We first crossed a bridge that was only one board wide, then passed a crematory where they burned the dead bodies and stopped to look at the coffins that were black from human oils.

During the autumn there was Tanabata *matsuri*.[1] That night the men and women *kamisama* [Shinto gods] met. We would light candles and offer melons, eggplants, and make *somen* (Japanese vermicelli). Tenjin-san *matsuri* was the festival for the scholars' gods . . . ah, there were countless festivals for the myriad of Shinto shrines.

But the most happy time of the year was New Year. My parents' store was the busiest then too. There were many games to enjoy, food to feast on, and plays and movies to see. All year round there were festivals . . . my! how long I've been living. August 8 was the

O-bon festival [the Feast of Lanterns]. We bought lanterns and offered them at the grave site of our dead ancestors. After *O-bon* our family would take a three-day vacation to Itsukaichi or Hatsu-kaichi [seaside resorts], stopping at an inn along the seaside. Tired from swimming all day, we would rest on the cool bamboo mats and gaze out from the sliding doors of our room onto the calm sea while the maids busily prepared the evening's feast. When night crept in the insects began their symphony: The grasshopper would set a steady beat — "gi-chin, gi-chin, gi-chin," then the cricket would start "koro-koro-koro, koro-koro-koro," and the *suzumushi* (the bell-ring insect) would chime in with "chin-chiri-chin-chiri-chin-chiri."

Most of the time was spent going to school. Since my mother never went to school herself, her only concern was that we get an education. My parents thought that as long as they sent their children to school, they would get smart. I went to a Buddhist school. That's why from when I was young, I was deeply steeped in religion. The schoolmaster was a priest named Nagai Ryujin.

I attended six years of elementary school: two years of *Kōtō shō gakkō* [middle advanced elementary school], and four years of girls' middle school.[2] We studied English and Japanese, mathematics, literature, writing, and religion. They taught us things of obedience — to obey a person's order. They also taught us womanly things: Women do not stand above men and flaunt their authority; in the house the man is the most important person; a woman must raise her husband up in front of others. But the most important thing that they taught us was religion, for a person who has religion is the happiest. On January 15 through January 16, the day that Shinran Shonin[3] died, I would go by myself to listen to sermons from morning until night.

In those days one could become a teacher after graduating from girls' middle school. Very few were privileged enough to go. I had three best friends: Miyamoto-san, whose father owned a cement factory; Mori-san, whose father owned a prefectural hospital in a quiet place called Kako Machi; and Miyakawa-san. She was from a poor family. She would say to me, "I talk but you don't understand my stories. All you think about is playing, but I'm thinking of making money when I get out of school."

Me? She was right . . . *tsumaran* [what a waste]! I didn't go to study. I just went to play. She used to say how lucky we were because we didn't have to worry about money. I understand her feelings now, and I often think of what she said to me. I never knew poverty when I was young. It was only after coming to America that I experienced suffering and I began to understand life.

2

MARRIAGE TO SABURO

*H*ashimoto-san always came to buy sugar at our store. She was a magnificent beauty with chalk-white skin and jet-black silky hair. She and her husband owned a small confectionery shop nearby. He was an alcoholic who often made a fool of himself and caused her much embarrassment.

One day she started telling us about her younger brother Saburo, who was living a troubled life back in her home village. She asked my mother if the Sato family could put him to work in their store. My mother listened quietly then replied, "If that is the case, bring him here and we will give him a job."

I remember the first time I saw him. He wore a *hanten* [a short kimono coat] wrapped at the waist with an *obi* [sash]. He didn't have anything to wear other than what he had on, so my mother gave him money to buy clothes. I didn't think too much about him then, other than that he was young and uneducated. But later, he was to become my husband.

He was only three years old when his father had left for America, leaving him and his two older sisters in Japan. His two sisters were true beauties. The younger one, Sachiko, was a *machi geisha*[4] who danced and sang, and played the *shamisen* (a Japanese banjo) at weddings and parties. She never did get married.

His mother, considered the most beautiful lady in Takata, had remarried after many years of never receiving work or money from her husband and had left her children with relatives. Papa[5] and his two sisters grew up going from one relative's place to the next until they were no longer welcomed. Even when he was starved with hunger, he wouldn't ask for food. His cousin would get a rice ball for him and he hid in the storehouse to eat. What a sorrowful childhood he led!

A person who hasn't suffered when he is young is no good because he knows nothing about money, but Papa suffered so much as a child that his mind was *hinekureta*[6] [twisted]. I used to think, how come I married a person like this? His thinking differed from mine. Me, I would listen to people and believe what they said. Him, he would say, "Even if they say such a thing to your face, behind your back they are saying something else." He would say things like that because he was raised by relatives. He grew up watching their faces, trying to figure out what they were thinking.

Papa came from a very good family line. There was even an assemblyman among them. But no matter how good the family, not too many people would take care of you for no money. It would have been different had his father sent something, but not one cent came from America. Who could raise you with good grace under those conditions? That's why Papa suffered. He went from place to place staying at each until they started to look disagreeable. He lived that way until he turned eighteen; then he came to work for us.

After he had worked for us for about two or three years, a letter came from America. It was from his father, telling him to come to America. Saburo first consulted with my mother. He regarded my parents as his own. My mother liked him because he was bright and industrious. She said, "If you want to . . . go ahead . . . but if you stay, we have a big business. I will let you run a part of the business by yourself." But when Papa decided that he would go, she got angry: "You don't have either parents. I thought of you as my own. But if you must, what can I do . . . go ahead!"

Papa left for America, arriving in San Francisco. When he first saw his father he thought, "Is this the stinking bastard! What a long time he made me suffer, never sending money home." The two stayed at the Aki Hotel in San Francisco. There they slept together for the night. Grandfather Tanaka kept trying to make conversation, even telling Papa how big he had become. Then at night as he watched his father soundly sleeping, he thought, "I should kill him for making me lead such a miserable life!"

Since Papa had suffered so long without money, he assiduously saved his earnings while his father gambled his. During those days the Issei all liked gambling. Takeyama-san had a gambling hall in the back of his barber shop and Grandfather Tanaka would go gamble there. Papa would wait patiently outside . . . midnight, one o'clock . . . but still he wouldn't come out. Papa would say, "Let's go home, let's go home." But his father would insist, "Wait, wait," and that's the way it went. That's how Papa got into gambling. His rationale was that as long as his father gambled so much, he might as well too. But despite that, Papa saved money.

Just about then World War I broke out. A fruit company in Liberty asked Papa's father if he wanted to go into partnership with them on their fruit crop: 30 acres of peaches and 30 acres of grapes. The fruit company needed a labor gang to pick their crop and that's why they asked Grandfather Tanaka, who could supply the men. Papa's father didn't have the money to pay for half of the investment that the fruit company wanted in advance. But Papa had saved his, so with his savings they went into partnership with the company and made a huge profit. They earned about $100,000 by selling their crop to the market back East. The fruit company took half and Papa and his father the other half. But there was still plenty for everyone.

Grandfather Tanaka then decided to go back to Japan, leaving Papa in America. He said, "You . . . you're still a young man. If I leave the money with you, you will spend it all. I'll take the money back to Japan and save it for you." With those departing words he left Papa stranded without a cent.

Papa was furious! He didn't want to see his father off. His father hadn't even left him with decent clothes to wear. But Papa's friend Yamada-san said, "You don't know . . . Japan is 7000 miles away. You may never see your father again. I'll loan you some clothes so you go." With borrowed clothes, horse and buggy, Papa went to see his father off. At the harbor Papa spit at the ship as it put out to sea. Not even a tear would flow.

Grandfather Tanaka returned to Japan. Loaded with money, he bought a resort home in Kure and seven and a half acres of mountain land in his home village. Hashimoto-san, his eldest daughter who came to buy sugar at our store, thought I would make a good wife for Papa, so Grandfather Tanaka came to ask for my hand in marriage to his son.

My parents were against the marriage at first. We were people of a fine, established house. Me, marry a hired hand? We wondered what kind of family would send their son to do work for others. But Grandfather Tanaka told my parents, "Come to the country. You live in Hiroshima and are a small business compared to us. Come to Takata and you will see; our family is old and established."

I went and visited their relatives. They all owned beautiful houses amidst many peach and persimmon trees. Land-wealthy from long ago, they were all of high social standing. My mother was embarrassed from the accusations she had leveled at them and finally consented to the marriage. She advised, "Marry his son because he came back from America with money — bought seven and a half acres of mountains packed tightly with cedar trees which will some day be yours." She thought they were wealthy and so did I.

When Grandfather Tanaka had returned from America, he was frightfully religious. He spent his days visiting temple after temple. He was a bright man and fluent in English so people would come to him to translate English. To his special guests he would serve coffee a little at a time. With an air of importance he bragged about American coffee and everyone would confirm, "*Ma-a-a,* how delicious it is."

Papa was still in America at the time but his father called him back. When he returned they argued constantly. Papa would tell me, "Twenty years he left . . . letting us suffer. Money I earned he acts like it's his own." I thought, what a quarrelsome household. In the Sato household my parents never fought.

We never had any cash and when I got married, my father didn't give me any. Your husband was supposed to give you money but Papa never did. To get money I sold all but two of my many fine silk kimonos. I couldn't ask my in-laws. My parents thought they were wealthy but they were only land-rich.

We stayed in Kure. The house was large with three bedrooms downstairs and three upstairs. We boarded only notable people: a naval officer, a government official. My mother-in-law lived with us too. What a fine person she was! Born into one of the wealthiest families in Kure, she was Grandfather Tanaka's second wife, whom he married after returning to Japan. She treated me just like one of her own although she herself was childless. When Grandfather Tanaka sold the house in Kure to the government, he said, "Let's go live in Takata," but she refused to live in the country. They separated and he returned to the country alone.

I kept coaxing Papa, "Let's go to America." I was on the adventurous side. I wasn't afraid of anything. I wanted to see foreign countries and besides I had consented to marriage with Papa because I had the dream of seeing America. I didn't care for him much . . . he didn't have much education. I could have married a real good person in Japan, but I wanted to see America and Papa was a way to get there.

Grandfather Tanaka said to us, "You have this much — mountains, means — America is not such a good place and besides, you may never be able to get back, so don't go." My mother wasn't happy that we were leaving, either. She said, if we stayed, she would give us the noodle shop that she had purchased and we could run it together.

But I kept urging Papa, "Let's go to America." I just couldn't wait to see it. We decided to go for a short while, make enough money for our trip, then return home. With that thought in mind, we borrowed $350 from Grandfather Tanaka and $150 from my parents and we left from Yokohama on the *Korea Maru*, bound for America. It was January 15, 1923.

3
COMING TO AMERICA
(1923–1925)

I was sick on the ship all the way to America. They fed us bread and butter. That was the first time I saw butter and just the sight of it made me sick. The ship was oppressively packed with people and the latrines were not like today's. We had to defecate into the ocean. When we stopped in Hawaii, I remember seeing funny things hanging in a store window. I never saw anything like it before. It struck me funny because of the shape — they were sausages. We never ate meat before. Meat was for *yotsu*[7] [a pejorative for Burakumin]. It was unheard of to eat meat.

About two weeks from the day we left Japan, we landed in San Francisco. From that moment on, I began to understand the world. We first went to the Aki Hotel and ate *miso shiru* (bean-paste soup), *iwashi* (sardines), and *daikon oroshi* (grated white radish). It was clean there. But when we came to Liberty (a town in northern California), the conditions were terrible. I thought America was supposed to be a beautiful, clean country, but it was dirtier than Japan.

We stayed at Ichikawa's boarding house. The walls were

plastered with pictures from magazines, the floors were dirt, and
there was only one bed. Papa said, "Well, this is it." From the
window I caught a glimpse of farmers in overalls shooting guns and I
thought, What an ugly place.

Liberty had a Japanese population of approximately 500 people,
of whom very few were women. Everyone knew Papa there and they
made a big fuss because he had come back with a wife. It was very
rare for a man to have a wife.[8]

After my initial encounter of *hakujin* (white) farmers in overalls, I
rarely saw another *hakujin*. From morning to night it was just
farming — no white faces. Papa would go out at night and come
home very late. At first I would wait patiently for him at the
boarding house. Well . . . evening glow and he still wouldn't come
back. I went looking for him. He was gambling. That was the first
time I saw a gambling hall — saw stacks of silver. They told me,
"Pull up a chair and play." There were many women there too.

Many of the Issei indulged in gambling. It took care of their spare
time. Papa was particularly good at gambling. When he played
hana [a Japanese card game], he knew what everyone had in their
hand. He just didn't know when to quit. He kept playing until he
lost everything. Once you indulge in a life of addiction, you never
quit: For Papa it became the most important thing in his life. I
began to think he was incurable.

We moved to the country to work at Kato's labor camp.[9] The
living conditions there were even worse. When it came time to sleep
. . . you know where we slept? On wooden boards cushioned with
hay and partitioned by a sheet. "Here you sleep," they said.
Ma-a . . . everyone could see us . . . a couple sleeping together —
sleeping next to others!

From there I worked continuously. I was the cook. That was the
first time I cooked, since my father's sister always prepared the
meals for us in Japan. During grape season there would be around
25 men to cook for. I was good. Everyone said my bean-paste soup
was the best and they came from all around to taste it.

Cooking was difficult at first because American food was
different. In Japan we used fish all the time but in America, Saturday meals consisted of steak (or pork chops — since it was cheap),

okazu [slices of meat sauteed with vegetables], or hamburger meat fried with noodles, and tomatoes. I experimented with an assortment of dishes because once the men ate it, they wanted new things to eat. I quickly learned how to make a variety of dishes.

Kato-san was a difficult man. He was the kind of person who would often caution others of their errors. Once I forgot to shut off the kitchen lamp when I went to the bathroom. He reprimanded me, telling me that I should shut it off when I wasn't using it. I remember that well . . . I remembered everything *tanin* [nonrelatives] said. I never did it again.

Kato-san got himself a wife from Japan. She was the younger sister of Yamada Kumaichi (Papa's friend). That woman was so good to me. She came from Shimane-ken. I remember when she first arrived. My, was she beautiful! She looked just like Nagako of the Imperial family when she was young. I never cast my eyes on such a beautiful woman — so graceful and slender. She had one child with Kato-san and about a year later, he died.

That morning he was to go fishing. I made a lunch for him and brought it to him. He was dead. His wife lay sleeping with him and didn't even know he was dead. His dog, named Dick, must have known better because he barked throughout the night. The dog would fetch the paper for him each morning but that night his master had died of a heart attack in his sleep. His wife returned to Shimane-ken. During those days in the country, how could a woman get along?

After that, Papa's friend, Yamada Kumaichi-san, came to run the camp. He was a living Buddha.[10] Yamada-san eventually called for a wife from Japan. This lady was short and squat — a real country hick — but what a beautiful soul. The more I got to know her, the more beautiful she became.

On the camp there were many little houses. There was Hanaki-san, who was there for so long: he's probably dead by now. Yamada-san's youngest brother also lived there. He was an extremely educated man but during those days, educated or not, you couldn't get a job if you were Japanese, so you helped out in the country.

After the grape-pruning season there was nothing to do so we would go to the asparagus camps in Stockton's Cannery Ranch. We washed and packed the asparagus into boxes for the canneries. Only Japanese did asparagus cutting. We lived in the wash house, lining up boxes and sleeping on top of them. The season lasted for three months from June through August. I remember how hard we worked . . . wearing boots all day long, stooping in the hot sun.

Everywhere we worked there were few married couples and the rest were single men. Those who had wives bragged. Consequently, the women without any children had many men pursuing them. A woman could take advantage of the situation and make good money. Yanagi-san did. She took up with other men because of financial problems.

Before Papa and I came to America the Issei were still able to secure wives through picture-bride marriages, but when that became prohibited[11] as well as immigration to America,[12] it left the majority of men without women. Many times men approached me and said, "Let me do it with you and I'll give you money," but I was hard — I never gave in. What an insult! I wasn't a whore. Once when Papa went to Utah to find gold, a friend of his propositioned me. "Let me do it with you," he begged. "You're crazy," I said. I told Papa when he came back. Papa was furious! That was the end of their friendship.

A woman couldn't show her charm to a man or he would think that she was giving him a signal to go further. And if she made him any promises she couldn't fulfill, her life was in danger. This waitress got her face badly cut with a knife because she would make promises to men that she had no intention of keeping after they had spent money on her.

Even false hope invited trouble. There was Ito-san, a married woman with one child, who became involved with a cook. He pleaded, "Let's get married," but she said, "How could I. I'm already married." Then he proposed to her, "Let's die together." She refused to do either with him so he shot her in the back with a pistol, then tried to take his own life only to discover there were no bullets left. He managed to find a rifle and went deep into the vineyards and shot himself. The daughter came home from school and found her mother dead.

After asparagus season, we returned to Liberty and I had my first child, Nesan. She was born January 1, 1924, at six in the evening. Tamura-san, the woman whose husband sold bean curd, was my midwife. In the country, doctors were not available, and when they were, either they would not treat us [Japanese] or their services were too expensive. So as a rule, the midwives substituted for doctors in delivery of the baby or the woman did it herself.

We made money washing and packing asparagus. We put about $2000 in the Sumitomo Bank and kept about $1000 on hand. Papa said let's go home because we had the fare and only one child. He said, "A country like America, it takes a long time to save money. We have been here one year and we have saved this much. We also have money back in Japan, so let's go home." But I didn't want to go back yet. I thought we could work just a little longer, make more money, then return home. It would have been bad to return without a lot of money. But after that time, we never had enough. No matter how much I tried to save, Papa would gamble it all away.

Pear picking started in Walnut Grove. I said, "Let's go." After pears came peach packing in Marysville. In Marysville the air was so stifling hot that we would arise at three in the morning and quickly pick the peaches before the sun's rays reached their peak. We lived in a vacated schoolhouse and fetched water from a well. Since there was no kitchen, we dug a hole in the earth and placed two metal bars over the hole to cook our food.

Apple packing came next, in Watsonville. I was the cook there. My, I did all the farm work there was to do in America . . . Papa and I and the children going from place to place. To move was easy. All I had to do was roll up the blankets and say, "Let's go," and soon after, we were gone. Issei — it was the same for all of them. They would bring their children everywhere. *"Sa-a!"* and they would wrap their children in blankets and go.

From Watsonville we moved on to Pismo. We stayed in a house behind a grocery store owned by a *hakujin* (white person). He felt sorry for us living in the camps and he let us live there free. It was the first time I lived in a house since coming to America. In the morning the waves would break, "Ja-a-h!" near our window. Papa would go fishing and we would dig for clams and cook them over the heat of a lamp. Oh, how delicious!

We worked for Masuoka-san picking peas. He planted them on the mountain's slope because they grew faster, away from the ocean fog, yet warmed from the gentle salt air. The view from the mountains was breathtaking. We would leave Nesan in the car and let her sleep while we picked peas on slopes so steep that you slipped with each step. Already my stomach bulged big with child. I worked up to the day Hana was born.

I remember when Hana arrived. The labor pains began late in the night. Papa drove me to the hospital in San Jose in a dilapidated Ford which barely made it over the hills. Each bump in the road sent a shock of excruciating pain. I gave birth before they had a chance to give me an enema. I stayed in the hospital for one week and came home to rest for another two.

I kept thinking, "I must work and go back to Japan." I was lonely — not a single relative. It might have been different had I been with someone I liked, but Papa never treated me gently. We never had conversation. We just worked and had babies.

Papa and I were not well suited for each other. He used to remind me that he wanted to marry his brother-in-law's daughter from a previous marriage. She was a rare beauty and a geisha, trained and quite accomplished in the arts. A person like that could have earned a living in America by teaching; Papa would have been well off. They would have been well suited to each other because Papa himself had an artist's spirit. He loved to entertain.

While in the company of others, Papa overflowed with laughter, but the minute he came home, he became *yakamashi* [stern, fault-finding]. At home he disciplined the children. He got angry if they used one word of English: "Use Japanese!" he admonished. "You go to school and learn English. A Japanese is no good unless he can speak Japanese." Even if I wanted to speak English, I couldn't. He wouldn't let me. "The children will naturally learn English," he said. Therefore at home they received discipline in Japanese: the language, social graces, practical wisdom.

He was severe. If I sat around not taking care of the household chores after coming home from work, he would say, "Don't go to work. After the household chores are taken care of, then go to work." He believed that a woman should never be idle for one minute. In the mornings, if I didn't come to the kitchen with my hair fixed neatly, he would get angry. Or if I came with slippers, he would say, "Go back into the bedroom and fix your hair and get dressed before you come out again." After marrying Papa, I have never risen after the sun was up. Even now, past four in the morning I can't stay in bed.

It has been that way between Papa and me ever since we got married. He never treated me well . . . birthdays . . . presents . . . clothes . . . who ever heard of such things? If I went into town, it was because my children were sick — not to have fun. But once I got married, I never entertained the thought of divorce. As long as he brought home enough to feed the children, I didn't care. Even if he was gone for a month, I didn't complain as long as my children could eat.

It's funny, you don't understand things when you're young. I always think now of how *oya fukō* [unfilial] I was. I'm *bachi ga ataru*[13] [suffering punishment] because my mother and father raised me and not even once did I return my *on* (obligation) to them. I was a bad person. I didn't even send a letter. I didn't even know when my mother died.

The reason I didn't write was because I was despondent. I was living such an abject life. I knew that my parents were well taken care of by my brothers and sisters. When I still lived in Liberty, a friend of my family's came to see me. He saw my mother in Japan and she wanted him to look me up. Mama worried about me. I felt bad. I didn't even write a letter to her. They knew in Japan that I wasn't living such a good life from the Saito's, who owned a barber shop and had returned to Japan. My Mama worried about me but all I could think about then was my children.

I keep thinking that even if my children are good to me, I don't deserve it because I wasn't good to my parents. I was *oya fukō*. I keep thinking about the mother-in-law in Kure and about Papa's sister Sachiko. Both treated me so well. Sachiko, a single woman, kept her hopes in us that we would succeed in America and come back to take care of her. She was overjoyed when we got married.

But I hadn't forgotten about my relatives. I saved $350 and gave it to Papa to return to Japan, but he gambled it all away. As we made money, he gambled it. A woman can do nothing when her own husband gambles. You can't make things go the way you want. The Issei men all gambled . . . Papa loved it . . . I hated it.

But I was terrible. I sit in front of the *obutsudan* [Buddhist altar] and tell Hotokesama [Buddha] . . . confess all my sins. When I think back now, I can't lead a happy life in old age after doing what I did to my parents. During childhood, happiness is not really happiness because you are totally unaware of everything. I was stupid. I keep thinking *suman* [inexcusable]: I did wrong. But things just don't go as you plan in life. Life in America was so different from what I had imagined. Meanwhile I had given myself up to despair.

LETTER BACK HOME
(1925–1929)

*W*hat fun we had going to Los Angeles from Pismo! Our car broke down in the mountains and we stopped to fix it. We traveled with Abe-san. He was a college graduate — what a fine man. He felt sorry for us and he helped us get to Los Angeles.

Papa bought a truck and sold vegetables and flowers but the work wasn't continuous. Then he found a good partner and they both started landscaping gardens on Wilshire Boulevard. He knew nothing about gardening but he quickly learned. He would find rocks from the mountains and put any price on the plants.

We found a house on Kingsley. Naomi was born there. Suzuki-san helped me deliver her in the house. After her birth came a high fever that lasted for two weeks. I couldn't urinate and at night the fever would rise again. The doctor said it was a bladder infection. Suzuki-san helped again when Kenji was born. I thought it was another girl but it was my first son. Papa was very proud.

Kenji was still in my womb when I had strange feelings. That is why he's quick tempered. I feel sorry for him. Papa went out every night and gambled. I hated gambling with a passion. I hated even touching cards, but Papa loved it.

I worked at home making handkerchiefs, saving every last cent
for Kenji's birth. I pulled threads from the material, weaving various colored threads into the handkerchief until one o'clock each
morning. Secretly I hid the money so Papa wouldn't find it. After I
finally managed to save about $100 he discovered my hiding place. I
went crazy. A big fight ensued and I hit him so hard that my heart
stopped beating. I hit his chest and he slumped down into a chair.
He just sat there without speaking and I looked at him. I hurt him. I
felt so badly . . . but he had gambled all that money I was saving
for Kenji's birth. I thought to myself, no matter how angry I
become, I should never again hit anyone on the chest.

After that incident, Papa went to borrow money from the Saitos
— the sister of my older sister Haruko's husband. She went back to
Japan and told my parents how poor we were. Why did she have to
say that? I was going to pay her back.

We moved to the house of Murata on Vermont Avenue, a huge
place with four bedrooms. A couple had hanged themselves there
and people said it was haunted. But we lived there anyway because
it was free. Afraid to live there alone, I boarded some people. Who
could stay alone when Papa would leave, gambling for three, four
days at a time?

Kawada-san lived in the front room, Okada-san in the middle,
and we stayed in the other big room in the back. A gardener and his
friend boarded downstairs. Kawada-san ran a restaurant and eventually died of stomach cancer. Okada-san returned to Japan: A soft-
spoken, educated man, he wasn't the type to stay in America. My,
was he good looking! He used to do delivery for a Japanese store in
Los Angeles. I had never been in love with a man before . . . men
are demanding, but . . . the one man that I felt most fondly for was
Okada-san . . . because of him I was able to go on.

When there was nothing to eat but raw beans, Okada-san would
go out and buy food for us. He always worried about me. He saw the
pain that I suffered and one night when Papa came home with a
[Japanese] waitress after being gone for three days, he said to me, "I
feel pity looking at your existence. Here, this is money for you and
your children. Take it and go back to Japan." The waitress,
probably not knowing that Papa had a wife, got scared when she

saw me and said, "Take me home," but Papa told her, "Don't worry." I wasn't angry that he came home with a waitress. I was only infuriated when he gambled, but with women, he just drank and sang. He never had sexual relations with them. Of this I am absolutely sure.

I wrote a letter to Grandfather Tanaka asking him if I could return with my four children. I was going to leave Papa behind. He didn't want to go back just then. I should have returned when Nesan was born and when Papa said we had the fare to go back, but I was stupid — didn't know anything of the world. That's why I can't tell my children anything because I was stupid.

After waiting anxiously, the letter finally came from Japan. Grandfather Tanaka wrote back saying, "Know shame! . . . never sending money or anything. You are no longer part of our family. We cut our ties as parents. Don't step your foot twice on Japan. There's no home for you." He was angry because we never sent back the $350 we had borrowed. He had married a widow who had two high-school children, and they would look after him in his old age.

Papa was furious! From that time he changed. Until then he had planned to return home someday, but after that, he said he would never go home again. "My father is an *oni* [a demon]," he shouted. "Leaving me for 20 years to be pushed from place to place. He's not a proper parent, never thinking about his children. He is no longer my father. The mountain and land that he bought were purchased with money I earned."

It wasn't small money either. Papa showed me how much belonged to us. If Grandfather Tanaka was a good person, he couldn't have done what he did. Papa was right: he was not a good person. But Papa was also wrong. If he had thought about his sister, he would have sent her money. He was a man who sought after his own pleasures, and only someone like me could have put up with him. Grandfather Tanaka was right about one thing . . . it was shameful that we never sent money or wrote a letter. After that my hopes of returning home faded.

One night we quietly packed our things and left Los Angeles. The people who owned a chop suey restaurant on Tenth Street wanted to keep Nesan. Papa had borrowed money from them, and there was an implicit understanding that our debt would be erased if we gave her to them. They said, "If we raise her, she would be happy." They would take her everywhere, dress her in pretty clothes and a parasol. Nesan was a beautiful child. Everyone stopped her on the street to tell her how beautiful she was. The woman would sew her clothes, give her toys. The woman wanted an answer in the morning. We fled before morning could arrive. We went back to Liberty. I was angry. No matter how poor we were, I didn't give away my children.

5
HARD TIMES AHEAD
(1930–1942)

*W*e took a train from Los Angeles to Liberty. I was depressed because I hadn't menstruated for three months. As the train rumbled on at high speed, I sat drinking *miso shiru* [bean-paste soup] that I had prepared for the trip, and gazed out at the farmlands rushing past. I got up to go to the bathroom and "Po-TON!" Something came out . . . I was bleeding. I wiped myself with a tissue and looked. It was a fetus the size of my five fingers all curled up in a fetal position. The eyes were black and I saw its thing . . . it was a boy. He would have been my fifth child.

I always became depressed when I got pregnant because I couldn't work, and without work I couldn't feed my children. Once I remember pouring cold water over my stomach and even jumping off a peach tree, but I was healthy and couldn't abort. But I never thought of taking medicine to abort. I just thought of it as an act of *kamisama* [the gods].

Raising my children . . . that was all that filled my mind and watching them grow was my happiness. I used to wonder, Why is it that I have such good children? Everyone praised my children. They were always surprised at my children's good manners. "*Ma-a,* I've never seen children as well behaved as yours," they would say. Among my children, not a single one cried and didn't listen to me.

I would tell Nesan what to do, then leave for work. When we came home, dinner was prepared for us. My, how dangerous! I just left them alone and went to work, but if I didn't do that, we couldn't eat. Once when Kenji was still an infant, he fell out of bed. I came home and couldn't find him. I thought: How strange! Where is he? He lay under the bed sleeping. After that I put blankets under the bed so that if he fell, he wouldn't hurt himself.

I was *mucha kucha* [careless] with my children but *kamisama* looked after them. Not a single one got hurt . . . I was lucky. When I think of my children, I feel sorry for them. The way I raised them was unpardonable, regrettable. Despite the poverty they all faced, they all treat me so well with no resentment. It might have been good that they suffered. People don't understand life unless they suffer.

We stayed for a short time in Preston before moving back to Kettleman's, the place we lived shortly before we left Liberty. The country was better for my children. We could be tenant farmers . . . I could be the cook and there was always enough to eat. Chieko was born there at Kettleman's. Then there were my two sons Hiroji and Kozo, followed by another daughter Keiko. My . . . there were so many I have a hard time remembering.

Papa was the labor contractor and foreman at Kettleman's. He managed to secure the job because he spoke English. Papa gambled but when it came to work, he was serious and responsible. The bosses could depend on him. He studied long hours figuring out how he could grow the best grapes. He did his best; otherwise he wasn't satisfied. Me too, I'm very responsible when it comes to work. You know why? It's all because of Papa. That's what I learned from him. He would say, "No matter what kind of work it is, you must do it with the thought that this work, no one can do it better — no one can beat me." Even packing . . . he did the kind of work that made people say, "Ah, if Tanaka-san did it, we don't even have to inspect it." He was the kind of person who would get out of bed even in the middle of the night if it were raining, and bring in the grapes set outside. No one complained about his work. For him, a way to do things better and quicker always existed and he would find the way. That's the kind of person he was when it came to work.

I have that nature too. I do the kind of work that no one can complain about. I have worked all these years without one complaint. I always figured out how to do the best work possible. I think and work . . . how can I work the fastest and do the best work? I worked faster than two people combined. Even with asparagus, I figured out how I could cut it faster and pack it neater than anyone else. Others would get a little at a time. I would do it faster. Even with grapes I did the same.

I'm fast . . . but there were some who were even quicker. Picking strawberries . . . the one who brings the crate out first is the fastest. I would have only four baskets picked and some people would already be carrying their crate out. It was all piecework — you got paid by the number of crates you picked. Hana worked the fastest, even though she was still a young teenager. No one beat her. Pruning . . . strawberries . . . her hands were fast. She left all the young men far behind her.

Contract labor . . . you earn money . . . thousands . . . but Papa gambled and that's why we never had any money no matter how hard I worked. Not just anyone could have done the work I did. I sometimes cooked for as many as 50 men (all Japanese) with three big pots . . . rice, *okazu* [meat sauteed with vegetables], *tsukemono* [pickled vegetables], and other dishes. Before I went out to the fields to work in the morning, I would have the food set out so that when I came home, it was all ready to cook.

When the grapes got ripe we hired men to pick them. Nothing was worse than no work . . . but as long as we stayed at Kettleman's, we could eat. It was the Depression then: Hoover was president and we had prohibition. But we didn't have it so bad. People on either side of us went bankrupt. They couldn't pay their workers. The grapes rotted on the vine. All the rich landowners went broke — only Kettleman's remained.

We grew peaches, prunes, and grapes. A large ranch, *neh?* Winter — pruning; summer — watering the ranch. The money was good. All year round five or six men worked for us, and during the grape season we hired at least twenty-two. I always cooked for the men, and when grape season came I packed the grapes because then the crates would pass inspection.

One season, after working at Kettleman's for about six years, we had a bad grape crop. When grapes were bad, Papa gambled more in an effort to recoup our losses. One evening Papa went to town, saying that he was going to cash a check. The check was a large amount with which he had to pay all his workers. I should have gone with him, but I didn't because the men were hungry. Busy cooking, I kept thinking, "Ah, he should return pretty soon." All the men were dressed up, ready to go to town and just waiting for their money. I fed them all and even washed the dishes. I kept looking at the clock but he still didn't return. I told the workers that I would go to town and find out what happened to Papa. I found him in the gambling hall. What could I do? He had lost all the money.

I borrowed money from the gambling hall to pay the workers. I managed to pay all but three. Omi-san was one of them. He said, "Pay me next year when things are better," but the remaining two told the boss. Mr. Kettleman got angry. "Leave!" he said, "I don't like people who do things like that."

Papa left the camp telling me to handle things. He said he was going to Terminus to make money, but that was a lie. He just ran away until things cooled down. Late at night he would sneak back to the house and peer through the windows to catch a glimpse of us. He was unshaven — living like a hobo. We lived without him for two months.

I can't begin to explain how much I suffered at that time. When real poverty sets in, that's when courage takes a back seat. The meat man, the fish man . . . they all stopped coming. The children and I would go to the tomato ranch to pick the leftovers and collect the beans that were thrown away by the neighbors. That all happened because I was stupid . . . but I grew up. I learned about being poor. [By this time, Mama was 31 years old and had eight children.]

We moved next to Shimono's. It was a shack, shaded under a big oak tree. The rain seeped in through the cracks and the wind blew the roof up from its foundation. We would cut the grape vines and burn the cuttings in the stove to keep warm from the relentless chill. We had no running water either. We pumped our own water, cooked outside, and bought a sheep for its milk. People said, "Go on welfare," but we didn't. Papa didn't want to. He thought it was *haji* [shame] to do such a thing.

We had to make money somehow. There was no work — no tomorrow money. Papa didn't like to work for other people unless he got hired as the foreman. Instead he would go fishing from early in the morning, taking Kenji with him.

With my children, I worked. My, how I worked. That's how I got old. But my body was healthy and not once did I get ill. No one worked more than I: work that seemed impossible, I did. I remember clearing 40 acres . . . or maybe more . . . as far as the eye could see. They wanted all the brush burnt so I did it by myself, taking my children along with me . . . gathering, then burning; gathering, then burning. When you are young, you can do hard work. When you are young, you do things unthinkingly.

Yoko was born under that big oak tree. Since we were too poor to go to the hospital, I thought I would deliver the baby myself. I asked our neighbor, Esaki-san, if she would come and help me — I would give her instructions. The baby came out with the water. I carefully pulled the baby out and cut the umbilical cord. The cord looks like intestines and there are times the cord slips back in so you have to tie and cut it between the two ties. I began to massage my stomach. It hurt but I kept massaging until all the afterbirth came out. It was the size of a cantaloupe. Then the blood kept flowing. Esaki-san washed the baby for me with hot water. I folded the cord and pressed it in. The cord later gets hard and falls off, but until then, I would put vaseline on it.

Children are difficult to bear but I never let out a sound. I would hold the bed rails and think that even if I die, it must come out. In San Luis Obispo, where Hana was born, the *hakujin* [white] women would scream, "Hurry, come, I'm dying!" They have low tolerance for pain. I never let out a scream even once with all the children I had.

Nobody knew when I was pregnant because I carried small. From the fifth month I wrapped my stomach with a cotton cloth. In Japan they say, "Bear small, raise big." In America they say, "Carry big and raise big." The labor pains with boys are different: They come fast. Girls go *"jiwari . . . jiwari . . . jiwari"* . . . I guess girls are weaker after all.

After giving birth, I didn't work for a month. Papa would carry heavy things and do the work. In Japan that's the way it was. They believe that your blood changes and if you do not take care of your body, you get sick, especially in old age.

The most sorrowful time during that period of hardship (1930–1942) was when Hiroji and Kozo died. I killed them. I treated them *mucha* [carelessly] . . . they must resent me. I will never forget the two. Hiroji and Kozo . . . even though they were male children, they never gave me trouble. What do you think of that? Kozo, he was so good. I would come home and he would be pumping: *"Ga-chin PUN! Ga-chin PUN! . . ."* then, *"jiri-jiri-jiri,"* the water would trickle out. It took all day to pump 50 gallons.

Before I went to work, the boys would prepare everything at home, then go to work with me. They would pick up the thinnings, put them in a wagon, and follow me while I worked. Once Hiroji tried to reach in a box to get some almonds and the entire box fell on his head, splitting open a big gash. He never let out a cry.

Two or three days before Kozo died, he sat under a tree silently watching me work. Even now I see his face watching me. He had a strange look on his face. He ate so many green grapes. The doctors misdiagnosed his case as the flu but it was dysentery. He died at the age of three when we still lived at Kettleman's Ranch. Hiroji died a year later of tonsillitis at the oak-tree house. He was only six. I killed them both by taking them to the hospital only when they were practically dead; we had no money.

Kenji almost died too, of rheumatic fever. His temperature was 106 degrees — only the whites of his eyes showed. I called the doctor but he said he wouldn't come. I called Yamada-san and he said to put him in the hospital immediately. He would take out the money. I didn't even have a sweater to wear to take him to the hospital. If I didn't take him, he would have died too. In Buddhism they say that if it's written in your fate, you die.

Yamada Kumaichi-san — a man of all men. He was the one we knew since coming to America. I have never met a man of such fine character in America. When Hiroji and Kozo died, we didn't have money for a funeral. Yamada-san said you have to have a funeral. He had twenty men working for him. He went to them and said, "I want you all to contribute some *kōden* [a monetary offering to a departed spirit]," and they did. Since I didn't have a black dress to wear to the funeral, his wife gave me one. I kept it in the trunk to remind me of her kindness.

Yamada-san never mentioned to anyone how well he treated us. He was a living *hotoke* [Buddha]. When we first returned to Liberty from Los Angeles, Yamada-san let us stay with him and we slept in the kitchen. It was stocked with rice and soy sauce. When one of the workers accused us of eating all the food, Yamada-san responded, "I have it for them to eat."

When Papa would go down to the cellar to drink *sake* [rice wine], the same worker would say, "Lock the cellar!" Yamada would reply, "Let him drink all he wants. I have over a hundred gallons. He couldn't possibly drink that much." To show my gratitude, I would make *sushi* [rice cakes] and bring them to the missis, but she would tell me not to do such things.

Yamada-san came to our rescue again when Papa totally smashed up our car while we were still at Kettleman's ranch. Papa often got into accidents, barely missing death by an inch and walking away from each with only a bruise or a cut. But this time he really hurt himself. That night I stayed up worrying because he didn't come home. I paced the front yard, waiting for him to return. In the early morning he came trudging home with blood encrusted on his face. He had rammed the pick-up truck into a tree on his way home from a drunken night of gambling. When he regained consciousness, he thought he was dead. The truck was wrapped around the tree and smashed beyond recognition.

Papa had hit his chest against the steering wheel but he refused to go to the doctor. Instead, he complained every year thereafter about his chest. I was just grateful that he was alive but we needed that truck to bring the men to work on the jobs that Papa secured. Without it, we couldn't work.

We had no choice but to turn to Yamada-san for a loan. Papa couldn't go and ask because he wouldn't have gotten it. Instead, I went. I had to go or we couldn't eat the next day, and I was pregnant again. I walked all the way to Yamada-san's alone. The night was country black and the dogs kept barking at the sense of a stranger's intrusion. As I passed a bridge, the lure of the rushing river caught my eye and I stopped for a moment thinking it might be better if I were dead. Life was too difficult. It would have been easier to die. But I summoned my courage — only small people took their lives. Besides, people would laugh and my children would suffer. I felt helpless, for I was pregnant; and when a woman is pregnant, she has no power — she's at the mercy of her man because she can't work.

When I reached Yamada-san's house, I stood outside trying to gather enough courage to knock. The fragrance of the chrysanthemums that Yamada-san nursed with such pride wafted through the night air, intensifying the sadness I felt inside. The chrysanthemum is the *mon* [crest] of the Emperor of Japan — the pride of all Japanese — and yet there I stood, ready to ask the most difficult thing that my pride would allow.

I knocked and entered. Holding my head very low, I asked for the loan. Yamada-san consented. He loaned us $300, and in those days, you could buy a new car for that much. He said, "You need food to eat too, so go to the grocery store tomorrow and I'll pay for it." Even after Papa failed at Kettleman's and everyone stopped coming because they thought we would ask to borrow money, Yamada-san came to tell us he would loan us money for groceries.

It was New Year's day when Yamada Kumaichi-san decided to return to Japan. Papa went fishing and came back with a big fish. We had $80 and I brought it to him along with the fish. He said, "From now it gets cold . . . then pruning. You have all those children to feed. I don't want this money." Pressing the money into his hands, I pleaded, "I'm grateful for your help and I've saved this money with the intention of returning it to you." He threw it on the floor and told me, "I earned enough money. I don't want to return to Japan with money you suffered so much to save. I gave it to you. Don't think you borrowed it. If your children succeed one day, then return it."

I couldn't stop crying. I told him, "I am *giri gatai* [a person who has a sense of duty, gratitude]. I can't take it back." He sat there still thinking. Slowly he responded, "Then when I return to Japan, I will give $40 to Sato's family and $40 to Tanaka's." I was overwhelmed by his kindness. That was the first time I sent any money home.

Yamada-san went back to Japan and was returning to America via Shanghai when he died. *Bachi ga attata* [I am being punished by heaven]. Papa always said Yamada Kumaichi-san was so good. I owe him the most *on* (debt) of anyone in America. Under his assistance we came this far and I was never able to repay my *on* to him. I can't say anything bad about anyone.

Sakata-san was one of Papa's best friends. He owned a chop suey restaurant in Liberty's Japanese town, where he lost money every day. People just didn't come in . . . besides, he wasn't a businessman. He bought the restaurant in order to find out how his youngest brother was killed. He knew that the restaurant would attract many *yakuza* (gangster) types who could provide him with information about his brother's death. He discovered that his brother was killed after gambling in the Tokyo Club. He had cleaned out the club of all the money it had. They said, "Put down the money and bet it," but he walked out with it and they killed him.

Sakata-san sued the club. He lost the suit and in the process lost all his land and even his house. Sakata-san owned some hundred acres of farmland. He was so rich that he never went to work for anyone else. Huh! Men do funny things. After he lost everything he owned, he would go fishing with Papa. He was so embarrassed to sell the fish that Papa would go alone then split the profits. Papa didn't care.

Sakata-san told Papa, "I'll give the chop suey place to you for free. Just take it over." When we took over the place, it started to do very well. But Papa loved to drink and gamble and that's where all our earnings went. They gambled in the back of the restaurant. I used to feel terrible when people from the country came and lost their money. Gambling is a terrible thing . . . I hate it. That's why I couldn't stand the chop suey restaurant. Only rogues frequented the place. Nesan helped in the restaurant and I swore she wouldn't marry anyone who patronized the place. I kept thinking about selling it.

We moved to a small house near Yamamoto-san's farm. It was much better. I had two more daughters there: Midori and Harumi, Yamamoto-san visited us every morning. He was almost blind but even in the rain he would come. I can still hear the sound of his boots in the rain . . . *"jabu-jabu-jabu, jabu-jabu-jabu."* I would look forward to his visits.

Near Yamamoto-san's farm there were 30 acres that the owners wanted to sell for $3000 because of bad drainage. Yamamoto-san kept urging us to buy it. "I'll loan you the money," he said. He wanted Nesan for his only son but she was still young and we depended on her help.

We finally sold the chop suey place. One night a couple of federal agents entered our place. In the back they were playing *hana* [a Japanese card game]. During those days every business had gambling in the back and sold liquor without a license but the police allowed it. I should have smashed the bottles of *unkappe* [a Chinese home-brewed liquor] that we had stored upstairs, but instead I hid it in the alleyway and they found it . . . I was stupid.

Papa gave $100 to one agent, telling him to split it with his partner. Those days people were always paying off the police so that they could gamble and drink without harassment. But Papa shouldn't have given them money since he had never seen the two before. Ochida-san, Papa's good friend, told them, "They have a big family. Take me instead." He was a *yakuza* [ganster] — he didn't have a family.

We couldn't afford to hire a lawyer. Papa represented himself, bringing all his children (nine) with him to court with the hope that the judge would be more lenient. It didn't help. He was sentenced for bribing a federal agent. The sentence was either 15 years in prison or a $10,000 fine. We didn't have that kind of money so Papa was sent to San Quentin. In those days Issei were sent to prison easily. They didn't have a chance. But at least Papa didn't go to prison for stealing . . . he never did that.

In San Quentin Papa studied and became fluent in English. Before that time he knew very little but he was bright and quick to learn. He only finished grammar school but when it came to talking . . . *ma-a!* You know the university students that came to work for us during the summers? He could outsmart them with knowledge. He would always say, "If I only had schooling like you, I could have been a lawyer." It was sad. He didn't have education, but he read a lot of books. He was glib with words. A countless number of times he wanted to throw away the pruning shears and study.

In San Quentin Papa also learned about *moxa* from a man named Tani, who was a *moxa* specialist in Japan. Tani-san once cured a prison guard by applying *moxa* and after that they allowed him to practice it in the prison. I would send it to them quite often. Whenever someone became ill, they called on Tani-san. He didn't charge a fee but would tell his patients that if they got well from his treatments, then they should pay him $50. Papa learned by watching him, and in Liberty people came to Papa for treatment. There was Tsutsumi-san who couldn't even drink water, but after Papa applied *moxa,* she was well. It was amazing! You get cured immediately. There were many like her who came to Papa.

Papa stayed in San Quentin for about a year. When he was there it was easy for me. The government gave me money for my children. I used to think that he should always stay there. The doctors were free. If he would only stay a little longer . . . I didn't worry about living.

6

THE WAR YEARS (1942–1944)

*W*e sold the chop suey place for $1000 and one month later the War broke out; the Nakatas who bought the restaurant lost money. It was heaven's rescue because now we had money. They sent us to Stockton Assembly Center, which was horse stables temporarily converted for our internment until the permanent camps were established in Arkansas.

My daughter Hiromi was born there and shortly after, Papa came back from San Quentin with the help of some Christian people. They argued that it was unjust that he was sent to San Quentin for doing what he did: everyone was gambling and selling liquor without a license.

We stayed in Stockton Assembly Center for two or three months until the camps in Arkansas were ready. We traveled there by train with the shades drawn down. It was better that way because quite a few Japanese people were killed by Americans before we were interned.

People closely affiliated with Japan were rounded up and imprisoned earlier. There was a young Japanese man in our town who told the FBI everything. He received money for being a rat.

People said after the war they would kill him. The FBI also approached me and offered to pay me money but I said, "What are you talking about! You're crazy!" But that young man told. I would never do anything like that — tell on others to pull them down. Even if your mouth is rotten, you should never be a spy. No matter how poor I was, even if I couldn't eat tomorrow, I could not be that rotten. My lips were sealed tightly but there were people who told. A person must be human. You can't say things about others that would bring them down . . . even for money.

My biggest worry had been money for food and shelter. In camp that burden was wiped out. The government fed us and gave us a monthly allowance of $10.50. Food came out from early morning. The camp was divided into blocks and each block had a big kitchen. Everyone lined up to eat in the mess hall. Do you know what they fed us at the beginning? Corned beef and cabbage every day. Then it slowly changed.

People tried to think of things to occupy their spare time. There were English classes, flower-arrangement classes, and dance classes. They asked me to teach Japanese, but I didn't because I was pregnant again. It looks bad when you're already old and pregnant. [Mama was 40 years old at the time.] The pregnancy was hard on me physically but I had nothing but good thoughts.

One day our block would have a talent show, the next day a different block. Papa got pulled from block to block. They called for him constantly. He was never home to fight with. What an actor he was! When they did plays, he would always perform in them. No one could sing *Yasuki Bushi* [a Japanese folk song] better than he: Everybody said that. He would sing among thousands . . . even a professional would have run away barefooted from stage fright. When I was young . . . I always remember thinking how good he was.

The winters were cold, but we had a big stove. A fire was always burning. People went to the mountains and collected wood. They carved and polished the wood, making *obutsudans* [Buddhist altars], drawers, chairs, all sorts of things. No matter which way you faced, there were mountains. You couldn't tell which direction was east or west. Many got lost and search parties went out to look for them. There were quite a few who died there.

I grew vegetables. Everyone grew them in front of their barracks. Watermelons, eggplants, sweet potatoes . . . everything grew well. The soil was rich because no one had grown things there before. That's why Papa wanted to stay and farm.

There were two factions in camp: one who said they would stay in America, and another who said they wanted to return to Japan. About half returned to Japan.[14] I didn't want to return to Japan. America was my home. I know I made the right decision.

In camp the Yamaguchis asked for Nesan. There were many seekers after her hand in marriage. But we knew the Yamaguchis back in Liberty. Everyone knew the Yamaguchis. There were *bigu shatsu* [big shots]. Although they were one of the wealthiest families in Liberty, we didn't gain anything from the marriage: we just lost a daughter.

We couldn't have a real wedding because it was camp time. Just the immediate relatives attended. I think Hana got married to the Maedas in camp too, but I can't remember any more.

Before the War ended, we left the camp with the Yamaguchis. We promised that we would grow food toward the war effort and they let us go. Several families left at the same time. We were already there for two years.

We left camp and leased 100 acres in Little Rock from a man called Glenn Stewart. We leased 30 acres and the Yamaguchis leased 70; they lost money, but we prospered. We grew green onions, carrots, beans, tomatoes, and okra. We sold the produce in the market place and managed to save well over $20,000. I didn't want to leave.

Hakujin [whites] from all around would ask us to work their farms. We hired two or three *kurombo* [blacks] for 25¢ an hour. They all wanted to leave and come West because work was scarce. We plowed the fields with a horse and I cultivated each row by hand. I did much of the field work by myself, working late into the night peeling, washing, and bundling the vegetables. In the morning Papa went to the market, either Safeway or Kroger, and came back with the money by nine. Before we arrived, the markets bought their produce from California growers, but since ours was fresher, they bought from us.

Glenn Stewart owned a broom factory. I wonder if he is dead by now? Even after we returned to California, he kept writing and asking us to return and buy the land. He couldn't farm the land himself because his business kept him too busy. On Christmas he would come with $100 in dollar bills and pull the bills out one by one to give to the children. He even gave us a car so that we could go to the market and sell our crop.

No *hakujin* (white) was that kind in California. There was also Mr. Manning, the wealthiest man in Little Rock, who cried when we left. He warned us that we would suffer in California. He told us that we were stupid to leave because opportunity to make money was unlimited in Arkansas. Another *hakujin,* Mr. Kern, said he would give us 10 to 20 acres if we stayed: together we could make money. We couldn't lose. They gave us a farewell dinner before we left. The *hakujin* in Arkansas treated us like relatives. If I were younger, I would go back. They're not like the ones here in California.

Looking at the children's future, we knew we had to return to California. If we stayed, the girls would have ended up marrying either *kurombo* [blacks] or *hakujin.* Papa and I decided that we couldn't just think about ourselves — with this money we must return. And with one truck and a station wagon, we left when we were ahead . . . a person's fate is determined.

We left when it looked as though the War had ended. The Yamaguchis left before us. They had land in Preston. They had made their biggest mistake when they sold 150 acres of prime land along the highway to some Italians who kept insisting that they sell. But they hung on to the 500 acres that they had in Preston.

Yamaguchi was a smart man. Taikō Yamaguchi [*Taikō* was a title taken by Toyotomi Hideyoshi,[15] literally His Highness] — no wonder they called him that. Everyone sold their land when the War broke out and we knew we were going to camps, but Yamaguchi bought 1000 acres. I could hear them cultivating the land all the way from our house.

Taikō Yamaguchi . . . he had the value of that name. He had the courage of Toyotomi Hideyoshi, the son of a farmer — short like Yamaguchi — who united Japan and then looked to Korea. That's how his behavior differed from the Tokugawa.[16] The Tokugawa didn't think of Japan — just themselves. That's why Japan was so backward. They were isolated but in the end great men like Takasugi Shinsaku[17] and Itō Hirobumi[18] had the insight to bring Japan forth, change her, and take her into the modern world.

Yamaguchi was like those men. He didn't think small, even when he was penniless. He had grand ideas, big courage . . . a real *yarite* [capable person]. There are no more like him . . . no one with as much courage and generosity.

7
LIBERTY, CALIFORNIA (1947–1956)

Coming back from Camp, we went to Preston and worked at the Mettler's ranch. We called that place the Tin House because it was built out of corrugated tin. It was one large building with the bedrooms upstairs and the kitchen below, with the bathhouse located in a separate building in the back.

It was at the Tin House that Naomi decided to move to San Francisco. She had been living in and working for a minister's family while we were in Arkansas, and when we came West, she had made up her mind to attend college in San Francisco. Papa was furious when she told him of her decision. He said, *"Katte ni se!* [Have your own way!] But don't come around again." Papa was like that. His rule among the children was that until you get married, you cannot leave the house.

Naomi was a different child . . . she was a tender, mellow person who never raised her voice. She left the house quietly with Papa yelling, "You have no parents or brothers or sisters!" When she arrived in San Francisco, she was so unhappy and lonely that she started to attend church and that's where she met Tadao-san. She

came back home one day to tell us that she was going to marry him.
Papa warned her that unless his family came to us respectfully he
could not consent to their marriage. He insisted that there be a
baishakunin [a go-between who checks out the prospective family's
background and arranges the marriage]. "After all," he said, "you
don't know if they're a horse or pig . . . we are not animals!"

When Tadao-san came with his mother and father to ask for
Naomi's hand in marriage, Papa gave in. At the engagement party,
Papa instantly took a liking to Tadao-san because he was very
perceptive. He kept filling Papa's glass with liquor: he knew how to
gain Papa's good humor. After that Papa stopped talking about a
baishakunin and Naomi arranged the wedding all by herself with
her own savings. It's no wonder she has no feelings for me. I didn't
do right by her as a parent.

We left the Tin House because with only 15 acres of grapes to
tend there was not enough work. We moved to the Smith's house
along Highway 99, where Kenji and Papa hired workers to pick
cherries and strawberries. We sold them at a stand along the
highway and earned as much as $200 in one day . . . but Papa
would lose it all gambling. After the cherry and strawberry season
was over, we sold corn and walnuts. But with a family our size, we
couldn't make ends meet and we moved again — this time to Payne's.

Shortly after our moving to Payne's, Chieko married Jim-san.
Jim-san had been asking for Chieko's hand in marriage for a long
time. He was a distant relative to Hana's in-laws, who had told him
that the Tanakas had good daughters raised according to strict
Japanese tradition. He came to our house and from the moment he
caught a glimpse of Chieko, he set his mind on marrying her.

Chieko was a true Japanese beauty and totally devoted to Papa.
She was a self-sufficient child and quick to anticipate others' wishes.
There were many seeking her hand in marriage but Jim-san was
determined to win her. Thereafter, his visits to Liberty were
frequent, and by taking Papa fishing he eagerly tried to win his
favor. Papa was fond of Jim-san, a generous and clever young man,
who had accumulated his wealth on his own by purchasing peach
crops after the War.

Their wedding was a very proper one. We traveled to Fresno with Nishimoto-san, our *baishakunin,* and our relatives. Jim-san's relatives were dressed in their finest clothes for the occasion. An elaborate spread of food awaited us and artfully packed in boxes for each guest to take home were fish, shrimp, *yokan* (sweet bean jelly), fish cakes, and a cooked vegetable and meat dish. The wedding ceremony was at the Buddhist temple, followed by a reception at a Chinese restaurant.

Before the wedding bonds are tied, each family's *baishakunin* makes visits to the other's family to discuss the wedding plans. The groom's *baishakunin* presents the bride with the *yuinō* [betrothal gift money], half of which she spends on making preparations for the wedding and the other half of which she brings to her husband's house after their marriage. In Japanese tradition the groom pays for everything, but for that reason the bride must bring her own quilts, a dresser, and various items for her own personal needs. There are some who say, just bring enough to stuff in a cloth wrapper.

Jim-san's *baishakunin* came with the betrothal gift money. He brought about $1000 but we didn't make any special preparations with that money. We just bought her a wedding dress and entrusted a little bit back to Jim-san. It didn't matter to him . . . he was in love.

Arranged marriages mediated by a *baishakunin* are good. The mediation binds the marriage well. If there is trouble in the marriage, the *baishakunin* tries to iron out the problems. The married couple is not free to do as they please, and when *tanin* (nonrelatives) intervene and give their judgment in a dispute, it holds great weight.

A *baishakunin* speaks on behalf of each family's interest and regards the young bride and groom as her or his own children. Our *baishakunin,* Nishimoto-san, extracted from Jim-san's family a promise that they would look after Chieko and treat her well. We gave her the *sake-sakana ryo* [wine-fish money] enclosed in a special envelope which she gave to Jim-san. After the wedding both families give money to the *baishakunin* for his/her services. We couldn't afford to give too much to Nishimoto-san but monetary compensation is not the reason a *baishakunin* offers his/her services — it's the honor. Nishimoto-san was especially good in her role. She was charming and had a skill with words.

At the Payne's farm Papa was the foreman. Mr. Payne really trusted him. The trouble with Papa was that if he didn't get along with the boss, he would quit even if he didn't know where he would get his next job. Not me . . . I would tolerate like a stupid fool. If I didn't like the job, or the boss, I would still stick to the job because I would have to think about the money. Never once did I have a boss say, "Go home." Even if the job was for a day, I worked like crazy.

At the Payne's I cooked for 50 men during the grape season and then went to work right along with them. The inspectors would open the boxes and if they were packed carelessly, they returned the entire load. Therefore the work had to be neat. I was good — a champion. I packed the grapes on top, the ones that they inspected.

No one beat me, even if I worked for others. Once when our shed was slow, two or three of us hired out to another shed to pack cucumbers. There was a bunch of *hakujin* (whites) . . . I worked faster than all of them. They got angry because I worked too fast and too neatly, so I quit. I wasn't going to work slow just because I made them look lazy. I thought to myself that when it came to doing farm work *hakujin* were stupid; *nihonjin* (Japanese) were all fast. You couldn't do the work without keeping alert. You had to be sharp . . . like Papa.

Mr. Payne owned his own grape company and other farmers contracted his company to pick, pack, and distribute their grapes. He had to know the exact yield of each grape crop and for that reason, he used to bring Papa with him to make the estimates. Papa would walk around, carefully inspect the grapes, and then tell Mr. Payne how much money the crop would yield. He was never wrong.

Papa contracted the workers and they picked the crop. We would pay them twenty to twenty-five cents a box and take a commission of about three to five cents above that amount. Besides the percentage that we made on the workers, we profited on the meals that we provided for them. With that profit, we were able to eat free. We used to earn about $5000 a grape season. After the season ended, we took the workers to other farms to harvest.

We always had a person or two who boarded free and stayed with us the year round. I never thought twice about feeding people. Only small-minded people feel bad about feeding others, but among the Tanakas, there was not one of us like that. I tried to save those who needed help. And for those who were penniless, I gave them some money to leave our place with. I never regretted doing things for others. Even if I was poor I tried to live each day with a rich spirit.

I particularly remember the holidays at the Paynes' because they were the best. I would get up early to look at the lights — even grown-ups like Christmas trees. Just about that time of year, Papa and I would be pruning the last ten or twenty acres, waking at four before the sunrise and working until after dark so that we could get paid.

When New Year's day arrived, Papa was jubilant. We spent several weeks preparing a feast that covered a table at least twelve feet long. Everyone helped to prepare it, even the workmen. They peeled the vegetables, watched the rice simmer, and pounded the steamed rice into cakes. Papa bought a mountain of *sashimi* (raw fish), chicken, and *kazunoko* [herring roe], spending at least $200. When it came to food, our Papa was very elaborate. If I didn't make enough, he would get angry, rush into the kitchen and start opening up cans . . . that's why I always had canned abalone on hand.

New Year's was the only day that the children and I did not have to attend to household chores or field work. All the children cleaned the house spotlessly and completed their unfinished chores on New Year's Eve so that they could greet the New Year with a clean start. As the neighbors and friends arrived to pay their respects, Papa poured the *sake* [rice wine]. Then after everyone was feeling warm from the *sake* and satisfied from the feast, he would sing his best songs and dance. Papa had that special talent for making people enjoy themselves. Me, I love people . . . I am good at getting on their good side, but from the time I was young, I never danced or sang. I never had a happy feeling where I felt like dancing.

Poor Kenji, his life was full of fighting with Papa from the time he was a young man. It was at Payne's that Kenji decided he was moving to Los Angeles to learn how to do body and fender work. He no longer wanted to work with Papa because everything they earned was gambled away. Papa earned big money — just to feed the children was expensive — but he always gambled until he lost everything. He loved gambling more than rice . . . that's why Kenji and Papa fought.

When Kenji told Papa that he was leaving, Papa was upset. "Don't come around," he said. "I could get along without you," but with only daughters left to help him, it was impossible. I was saddened. Without Kenji there wasn't anyone to keep Papa in line. So many times Papa would gamble money that wasn't even his to spend that I've thought of hanging myself, but I couldn't even do that.

After Kenji left, Papa was lonely. He was fed up . . . he was getting old and he no longer wanted to do contract farming. He couldn't do it by himself. Shortly after, Papa decided to buy a house in town: the first house we ever owned since coming to America.

December 27, 1953 — Papa died. He took off work that morning to go catch New Year's fish with Yamaguchi Nīsan (Nesan's husband), their six-year-old son Robert, and Grandfather "Taikō" Yamaguchi. The morning sky was clear and the air crisp but calm. By early afternoon a gale with winds ranging from 40 to 50 miles per hour arose unexpectedly and continued to threaten late into the afternoon.

Papa often came home after dark when he went fishing but never really late. We had just finished eating dinner when the knock came at the door. It was Papa's friend. A gust of wind accompanied him as he entered the house. There he stood, pale and speechless, as he realized from everyone's demeanor that we still hadn't heard about Papa's death. We all stood looking at him as he slowly broke the news: Their small boat had capsized and they were still missing. I knew they were dead.

We discovered the details of the accident from my grandson, the only survivor, who had stayed afloat with the help of air trapped in a windbreaker jacket that his father had made him wear. When the boat capsized, they all hung onto its sides. The currents were swift and the water too cold to swim ashore. A passerby had witnessed the accident but all the men had gone down by the time he could reach help. Papa was the last to go under. The last thing he said was, "Pull yourselves together. Hold fast!"

The morning Papa went fishing it was as though he knew he was going to die. He told me, "Please return the money we borrowed from the Sato house." Do you think he knew? How could he have known he would die? But it was as though he knew. He told me that he had come to live this long because a person like me had patiently stuck it out with him. He was grateful.

Papa may have liked to gamble and drink but when it came to the home and discipline of the children, he was strict. He stressed that a woman must be womanly. She must do for the man — be the keeper of the house. He was severe about things like that. He insisted that a woman rise early in the morning. *Mā-mā, neh* . . . I became a fine, disciplined person because of Papa. I'll tell you why. Papa never got up after the sun. I never slept in bed beyond the shining of the sun's first rays. He was severe. Even the morning before he died, he said, "Hey woman, get up, wake up!" The morning was still dark but he insisted that everyone wake up. He went to the children's rooms and woke them up.

After Papa died the children raised by me were not as disciplined. Everyone raised by me is spoiled; everyone raised under Papa is *shanto shitoru* [as straight as a ramrod]. But Papa raised children by complaining. This family was poor but the children's upbringing was admirable. They all had good manners. Papa would always say that you could tell about a family by watching their children.

I don't want to talk bad about Papa. He's a *hotokesama* (Buddha)[19] now. After he died, I couldn't blame him for gambling with all those children we had. He was always short of money . . . trying to make more by gambling. He could do anything even without money. People would set him up into different things. Papa wasn't an ordinary man. He was a man of courage, smart . . . if only he didn't gamble.

When Papa died we didn't have a cent for a funeral. What a problem! We called Jim-san that night and the next day he waited until the banks opened before he left Fresno. We waited for him . . . finally at midnight he came with $1000. We brought Papa home for him to see his house for the last time. In Japan the relatives wash the deceased's body down and dress him in a white kimono, but we had the undertakers do that and we dressed him in his only good suit, which we had purchased for Naomi's wedding.

The funeral for the three was to be combined into one. Since Yamaguchi-san was one of the largest financial contributors and active participants with the Buddhist Church in the area, the church had decided to pay for his casket. We went to see it. It cost $1,500 — the best one you could buy. Jim-san said that if Papa was the only one who had a cheap casket, it would be humiliating to our family. He took out the money to pay for it in addition to the other funeral expenses such as flowers. Papa adored Jim-san just as if he were his own son. I am forever obligated to him.

Ten Buddhist priests presided over the funeral. There was the head priest from San Francisco, one from Sacramento, another from Marysville, and all the outlying areas. Well over 1000 people attended, making up the continuous stream of cars which stretched from the Liberty Buddhist Church all the way to the graveyard. Never was there a funeral as large.

People from as far as Stockton and Sacramento sent us *kōden* [a monetary offering for a departed spirit]. We received about $3,500. I carefully recorded all the names of those who sent us offerings for in times of trouble in their households, I am obligated to return my debt of gratitude. The *kōden* was used to pay back Jim-san for the funeral expenses after which there was only $150 left. With that money we made donations to the Buddhist Church and other Japanese organizations. After that, we didn't have one cent.

Then Papa's insurance money came in: We got about $8,000. That's what saved us. After Papa died, I never experienced poverty. I no longer had to contend with a gambler. The unmarried children still remaining in the house were old enough so I didn't worry. (The youngest was nine years old and the oldest was one year out of high school and working full time.) I thought with humans you never know what can happen. One day Papa's fishing; the next day he's dead.

Shortly after Papa's death, Kenji got an honorable discharge from the army and came back to Liberty to help the family. He wanted to open a body and fender shop. "I have the tools," he said. "All I need is a place." I gave him $4000 to open the garage but he kept coming back asking for more. I told him that I couldn't because I had to set aside a little money for the rest of my children. Kenji wasn't a good businessman. He was too young, only 26.

Keiko (the eldest unmarried daughter still living in the household at the time of Papa's death) had a good head. She suggested, "Kenji keeps asking for money, so let's use it all. Let's buy a duplex or an apartment." One house that she took me to see is still stuck on my eyes . . . I can't forget it, even now. It had two houses on one lot with a big back yard to grow vegetables. There was also an apartment building that roomed about ten people. If we had bought that, I could be eating today without doing anything.

In 1956 we had to leave Liberty. I was saddened. We lived there so long . . . Papa and I. We would have stayed but Yoko left for Los Angeles, and without her, we couldn't get along because the rest of the children were still in school. I begged her to stay but she stole away in the night, saying she didn't want to live with us in Liberty.

She went to Los Angeles to follow Ted. She met him in Liberty. When he first came to see her at the house, Kenji got angry and told her to stop seeing him. His face was swollen and heavily scarred from birth, but what could you do . . . she liked him. Then too, he was Okinawan. People then thought Okinawans to be on the same level as Koreans.[20] But he wasn't a bad person.

I didn't want to sell the house: The payments were $45 a month. It would be mine by now but Kenji kept saying, "Come, come to Los Angeles." He said he couldn't make a living in Liberty. But look at him! Is he watching me now? He shouldn't have said anything. No matter how busy he is, can't he come once a month to visit? Up to now I have suffered . . . words cannot explain my suffering.

8

LIFE IN
THE CITY

*W*hen I was in Liberty I was dependent on everyone, but in Los Angeles I came to do things by myself. I was the pillar of the family. I had to bring home the money. If the main head of the house didn't work, how could the children be expected to work?

I found work right away. What kind of job do you think I got? A rotten job as a maid at Honda-san's hotel on Broadway. I worked three days a week. There were two maids and when they took off, I would work. That was the only job I could find. But regardless of what kind of work it was, I am a woman of the Meiji Era (1868–1912). I never looked at the clock and worked. I didn't stop until the job was finished.

I worked so well that he fired one maid and hired me. When Christmas came, I was upset. The salary was so low — I had to put my children through school! I just quit. He asked my why I quit, and I told him the pay was too low. I shouldn't have quit like that, though, because he fired someone to hire me.

I soon found work at University of Southern California preparing and serving food. The job was good but when summer vacation came, I was off for three months. I couldn't have a job that wasn't continuous. Then I went to work for Nakano-san at his hotel. He warned me, "This job is hard work." I told him, "Don't worry. I can handle it."

Those were hard days. Nakano-san's son kept quitting and coming back, but he was good to me and the nicer he was, the harder I worked. I left the house at six in the morning. I would sew and mend until 8:30; when people left for work I would clean their rooms, then sew again. I would come home at 6:30 in the evening, six days a week. If my health wasn't good, I couldn't have done that kind of work. I worked too much. No woman worked as hard as I.

I patiently worked for Nakano-san for 15 years. When there was another person to depend on, I didn't have to work like crazy. But I couldn't depend on anyone else. When I was in the country and Kenji wasn't married yet, I would combine my strength with his and do what he said. But when I came to Los Angeles, I felt like I could do it myself . . . independence came over me.

Hotel work was interesting. There was one *hakujin* [white] man who wanted to marry me. I laughed, "How ridiculous, I'm old enough to be your mother." He told me he had land in the country and he wanted to take me there, away from this dirty work. Then there was this Hawaiian. He had been after me to marry him for fifteen years now, but I wouldn't marry a person like that. Every weekend he went to Mexico to buy himself a whore. When he laid a hand on me, I pushed him away. I told him not to touch me with his diseased hands.

He lived at the hotel and followed me around all day and helped me. I didn't want him to. I told him, "You're a nuisance. How would it look to the other people?" I told Ichiro-san (the boss's son) that he is crazy, and when he would see the Hawaiian talking to me, he would laugh. Each night before I went home, he bought things for me: fruits, vegetables, cakes. He was only 45 years old.

Even now he calls me. He says that he has never met a person as kind-hearted as I, and that he wants to marry me just to be at my side. I tell him, "You . . . you think a little deeply. Between you and me, it's like a parent and child. What are you going to do living with me? I don't love you."

"Even if you don't love me, I love you," he persists. "Just let me be close to you. I won't sleep in the same bed. Just let me be in the same house."

"Are you kidding!" I tell him. "You, no matter if you love me or not, I will not marry you so you should give up." But he was a good friend . . . if I had asked to borrow money, he would have given it to me in a minute. I was like his mother.

He always carried ten $100 bills on his person. He had the cash just in case his parents should die and he would have to return to Hawaii. He showed me his bank book. He had $100,000 saved in it. "It's all yours," he said, "If we get married. We could take a trip around the world and settle down in a small town." I wouldn't marry a man like that for all the money in the world. I have a strong will. I wouldn't give in to that kind of temptation.

There were many men at the hotel who wanted to marry me. There was Fukuda-san, who had plenty of money. He was a tailor in Japanese town — a good person. He's dead now . . . went back to Japan and died. His mother used to tell me that she had known many people, but had never met anyone as good as me. She kept telling me that I shouldn't do work in a hotel like this. She died in the hotel.

There was also Masui-san. He had plenty of stocks. He could have lived on the interest alone. But I wouldn't give my body up just to gain money. That old man died. He kept asking me to look after him. Until he died he would sit all day where the sun hit him and watch me work. I used to clean his room for him. His health got worse and within one, two days, he died. He was a good person.

When you work in a hotel, there are plenty of people like that. I worked there for 15 years. There were many good men, but not even once did I give my body to them. I'm not that kind of person . . . I'm hard. I am not motivated by money. I am an honest person.

I never met a person there that I thought I would marry. I didn't want to either. I had the will to do it on my own. Besides, I had my children. I wanted them to be proud of me. Even when I was young and living in Los Angeles . . . there was a man named Hajime. He would always follow me around and ask me to marry him. But men are like that . . . they ask you to marry them even if they are already married.

You can find good people even in the most squalid places. For over fifteen years I have nursed people at the hotel. I took care of about ten who died. They were all grateful for my help. I would take them to the bathroom and they would offer me money, but I didn't do it for money. I enjoy being good to people. That's why I have been able to live a long healthy life.

Today is February 25, 1978. I awaken at four every morning. I study English for about twenty-five minutes, practice my ABC's. I lie in bed reading books and if there is anything good written in them, I write it down. I don't read novels. I just read about religion and health. The most interesting books for me are those concerned with health. I open the window and inhale the fresh air. Quietly I move my legs and massage myself, fall asleep again, wake up and lie in bed until six thinking about Hotokesama (Buddha) and how I will go to *gokuraku* (paradise).

When the man who lives upstairs goes to work, I always rise with him. That's about seven a.m. I get a cold towel, wipe my body, and do yoga for my neck, legs, abdomen, stomach — my entire body. I pull my ear lobes and press behind my ears: Those are exercises for good hearing. I press my eye sockets with three fingers. Then I massage my temples, pat the top of my head and the middle of my forehead, then massage the nape of my neck. You must do both right and left sides, back and front. You must to it regularly, not merely after things go wrong. I was thinking the other day how lucky I am . . . I have fewer aches and pains than a young person. After my exercises, I light the incense and pray to the Hotokesama. Then I take a short walk taking in the fresh air.

At nine a.m. I eat breakfast: tomatoes, cucumbers, carrots. I don't eat too much. I listen to the Japanese program on the radio, then wash clothes and do some cleaning. I take a nap at one in the afternoon, not really sleeping but resting. Again I read health books. For so long now I have recorded things from books; those are the things I read. Rheumatism, illnesses stemming from nervous disorders, those illnesses I have healed. When I was at the hotel, I healed many people. You do not get well overnight though. It takes a long time.

I would like to be able to do it for others, but I am too old now. I have healed so many of my own illnesses with diet, mind [spirit-soul], and exercise. Occasionally I go to Japanese town and speak to a group of old people, do *shiatsu* [accupressure], and discuss their health problems with them, suggesting several remedies.

Hiromi came over at 12:30; we ate lunch together. We sat and talked and she went home happy. She is a good person . . . we talked for a long time. I listened to her stories about her "old man" and I told her things she wanted to hear. The way she brags about him . . . how he is a *yarite* [capable doer]. After she left, I got back into bed and read. Then I did some more exercises. Even if you are in the house, you must do exercises. This is especially true for old people.

I ate at three today so now I will not eat any more. I will rest my stomach. The worst thing is to eat too much. Tonight I will watch Japanese television. I watch it until nine o'clock. My body is good now so my eyes shut by themselves. I sleep well. I have few worries. Worry is the worst thing — everything you eat turns to poison.

Some nights I get up and think from child to child and I can't sleep. I worry because I am a parent. When I look back, I think I was wrong . . . raising one child after another. They all suffered so much as children. We never gave them anything. From poverty they learned how to take care of themselves: Hana learned how to fix hair; Chieko too. That's why I think it wasn't too bad that they suffered somewhat.

I always think of when I was young and suffering with Papa . . . those were the best years of my life. I was with my children then. Now all my children are grown up and living on their own.

Children, you can't depend on them. From time to time I think that I should have done things to better myself because you can't live just for your children. Kenji, Kenji . . . look, he hardly has time to visit me. When I hear others say that their son did this and that for them, I am envious. It is only right that a son look after his parents. Daughters, the house they marry into is their place of obligation.

A child must not forget his parents — even if they gambled, they raised the child. The child must have enough feet to come and visit their parents. That's why parents should think of themselves while raising their children: because some children think that they raised themselves.

I can't complain about my son though. I wasn't able to do much for him as a parent. He is busy with a religion instead of doing bad deeds; that is good enough for me. Now Kenji says to come and live in the separate house he has in the back of his house. I can't go there. If he were sincere, he would keep coming to see me.

Daughters, daughers . . . they have their own lives and ways. If I went and curled up in their homes, I would feel sorry for them. Maybe I should just stay here and live by myself and when the time comes, go to the county hospital and die.

Now I think back about my mother and father. I was not good to them and I am suffering punishment. Look . . . with all the children I have, I live alone: That is my *bachi* [punishment]. Isn't that right? When you grow old, what is the saddest thing? Living alone. Don't you think I have come a long way? It is not easy being alone. You must have a strong will or you become defeated.

Without work I get sick of living. If I work, my mind is preoccupied and when I come home, all I have time to do is sleep. But staying home day after day . . . I'm sick of it. I don't have proper thoughts. I get lonely . . . tears come to my eyes when I sit here quietly by myself. It's not good to get old — you don't even want to run any more. Ideas don't match between old and young. The young have energy to run and exercise; the old sit back and watch. It is the most happy time when you are young.

Alone. It is sad. There is nowhere to go and no one to turn to. That's why the secret of success is to get along with others, to combine energies. Together with nature, together with each other's strength, we survive.

9

IMPORTANT LESSONS IN LIFE

I want to teach you an important lesson: The worst thing to do is show an angry face. You must show a happy face. If something gets you angry to the stomach, or you are very depressed, you should at least recognize another's presence; otherwise you are discourteous.

No matter how much education you have, you must have good manners. If someone comes over and you stomp around the house angry, what will they think when they go home? They would say, "My, that girl, what is wrong with her?" Our Papa always said, even if you fight to a point where you are both falling out the window, a woman must show a smiling face to other people.

You must look in the mirror and figure out how you can look more beautiful by smiling and having good thoughts. You can make others happy by smiling. The gods of wealth are always smiling. You can make a person want to try harder by being happy. My daughter Hana, she knows how to get along. She has an intuitive understanding about people. Midori is like that too. She knows how to make people like her. She will never starve. It is not education itself that gets you ahead: it is getting people to like you.

Buying clothes, eating well . . . that is not true happiness — it is making others happy. This neighbor lady, all she thinks about is making money. I give her things and she never returns them. You cannot always receive. You must return what you receive. To give is good: you receive more in return. When I go to Japanese Town, everyone wants to do things for me. I don't lose anything by giving and doing things for people. Instead, I gain more in return . . . I am happy.

My neighbor upstairs is always shining his car. The lady upstairs got angry at her son for standing on it. I said, "The kid could stand on the car. Where is he to play other than the streets?" That man has never offered to do anything for anybody. He is the only one in this building who owns a car, yet he has never offered once to do any errands for anybody.

No matter how much money you save — by saving it you will not save your name. There is a saying in Japan that "When a tiger dies his skin will be treasured; when a person dies his name will be remembered." Spending money only on yourself — what will a person enjoy? Money is a worthless commodity in itself. Some are crazy trying to make it. There are others who count their pennies and save each one. If you save money out of greed, it will run away from you, and that's the truth. You must look to save and help all living things. You must feel that others' happiness is your own. Even now I want to make money to help people. I want to be able to give all those people who suffer, those people who still have a future, a chance. That is my wish.

You cannot do anything unless it is combined with everybody's strength. That's why you must be grateful for everyone's effort. You must not forget those who came to your help in time of need. There are many people who think only of themselves. We must help one another and be grateful for their efforts or happiness will not come to us.

Humans are deep with sin. It is human nature to think that one's self is great. But you must think, "I must study even more, or what a worthless human am I." When you think you are good, that is when you are the most ignorant; when you think there is more to do, more to learn, that is when you are good. One must improve one's self, polish one's soul, experience various things, and learn. Until then you do not understand. That is moral training. That is what the Emperor Meiji said to teach the children.

Moral training does not exist now. That is what is sad about Japan today, for without it, Japan's behavior is disorganized. A country as small as Japan cannot be like that — cannot be loose in behavior like the United States or it will disappear from this earth.

If you raise children in the habit of being grateful to others, all through life they will be treated well by people. Dressing children in pretty clothes does not demonstrate a parent's love. The children's character is the most important. Only if your inner soul is *rippa* [fine] will you shine. It is not education that counts. People who are sarcastic and say, "Hey!" — they don't get the job. It's the soul that you have to discipline.

Beauty is seen in discipline. The *samurai* raised their children severely. They taught their children through righteous discipline. It is for the sake of the child. When children are young, they only know what their parents teach them. Buying things for them is not a parent's love. Parent's love is shown by building children's character, giving them values, and instilling discipline so that when they go out on their own, they will be fine people.

Three times praise and one time scold. They must go hand and hand. Praise and punishment . . . children do not understand otherwise. If they take something from someone else, you must spank them severely. But if they do good deeds for others, you must not forget to praise them. You will have it easy later if you raise them right.

The most important time is when they are young. A child's thought is developed by three, four. By nine it is all set. Until a child is eighteen and becomes free, he needs the discipline . . . to be told about the ways of life. The worst thing is a sarcastic child. Children must not talk back. You must teach them to respect their elders.

A female child is a blessing. Males are more difficult because they are mischievous. They think of themselves, try so hard to get ahead at no expense. A woman isn't like that. When I look at a woman with a male child, I do not envy her: I feel sorry. Male children look

to take money away from their parents. They do not say they will
look after their mothers, but girls do.

People who do not have children do not understand many things
about life. That is what you call *hisuteri* [hysteria]. Among women,
there are many. Even among men, there are some like the man who
lives upstairs. He is going blind and even then he hates to see people.

The most important thing to remember for a woman is her role:
to marry and raise children. To be happy is to have a good husband
and fine children.

Between husband and wife it is not enough to have love . . . the
meaning is deeper. That's why it is not good to get married young.
Me, I married without thinking. I looked at marriage in a shallow
light. I didn't like him much . . . I just wanted to come to America.
I was too young, and when you are young, your thoughts are thin.
But I never looked at another man while Papa was alive. Even after
. . . and there were many who wanted to marry me. My daughters
may be divorced but I continuously stayed married to Papa. I did
what I had to, forgetting about myself and doing for my children.

Once you marry someone it is forever. You must think like that —
that's how deep the meaning of marriage is. It is like religion: You
promise *kamisama* (god) that you marry until death do you part.
Promises are exchanged in front of *kamisama,* and if you divorce,
you break that vow. That's the purpose of a marriage in a church.

I'm saying things from the Meiji Era [1868–1912]. Today people
have different ideas. They do what makes them happy. When I
think of the Issei women . . . my, they really tolerated a
lot . . . putting up with men that made them sick to their stomachs.
But divorce was unheard of.

I think that I am to blame that my daughters are divorced. If
Papa were alive, nothing like this could have happened, but it is
because of me and the changing times. With Nesan as a model, how
can Yoko, Keiko, and Harumi divorce their husbands? They are the
dirt that accumulates under the fingernails . . .

Nesan is an image of the ideal woman. It is not good to brag
about your child, but anyone could write a book about her.
Widowed at 30, she stuck by her in-laws, put her children through
school, suffered for the sake of her children, and forgot about

herself. All those years for the sake of her children. My suffering is nothing compared to hers.

The others put themselves first, saying, "Oh, a person like that, how could I live with him?" What about their children? Look what's happening to them! My daughters' wills are too strong. They all think they could do it by themselves. But it is not too late to find happiness if they rectify from today — follow the path where they find no guilt.

Men are *wagamama* [selfish] though; that is why it is understandable why there are so many divorces. Men treated women like dirt . . . thinking it was enough just bring home the money. But that doesn't go any more. That's how it was in Japan. But I hear that even in Japan, women don't put up with all that any more. Each side is to blame — fifty-fifty — that's why it happens.

Look at Hiro. When Harumi mentioned divorce, Hiro said, "Once the thought escapes from your mouth, we can never get back together." This man must not have had much love for her. How much could he had loved her, having two children yet not wanting to reconcile just because she mentioned divorce once? But I don't know what Harumi was thinking about when she asked for a divorce. Hiro was not a bad man. Look at Papa, who gambled. I worried where the money was coming next, but I tolerated. That's why I think it is strange. What problems did they have? None compared to mine.

I think until you die a human must suffer. My daughters get divorced, Keiko gets sick . . . the suffering never stops. If Keiko wasn't divorced, I wouldn't worry because it would be her husband's and his parents' burden. But now it's back on me. That's why if you stay together with your husband, that is being filial.

Yoko didn't tell me about her divorce. Later she told me, "You don't have to worry. I'll never come to ask for money. I'll never burden you." She can say that, but look . . . I still worry. If Papa was alive, he wouldn't let her back in the house after her divorce. I'm so terribly sad to think my teaching led them astray. I am Mama so I let them come back, but I cry in my heart each time I do.

Ame ni mo makezu, kaze ni mo makezu [Neither the wind nor the rain will defeat me]: I want you to become that kind of person. You can if you are healthy . . . but a person is not worth a cheap novel if he does not have his health.

After Papa died, a doctor said I had cancer and unless I had my uterus removed, the cancer would spread to the rest of my body. I went to another doctor and he said that at the mouth of my cervix were two tumors. He pinched them off in his office. When he cut them off, he told me that before you know it, it will grow back. But look at me . . . I'm still alive.

My health got better from 50 after Papa died. Coming to Los Angeles I began to study about health. Especially after living alone, there was no one to look after me when I was ill, so through diet and exercise I figured out how to prevent sickness. From when I was young, I would eat and my stomach hurt. I thought I wouldn't live past 60, so I started to study: *shiatsu* [a form of acupressure], *moxa,* acupuncture, health through diet.

I could look at people and right away know about their health. I have extensive experience at diagnosing illnesses. I watch people as they enter the bus, and immediately I know what's wrong with them. A person's legs are swollen when the kidney and liver are not functioning properly. One-third of a person's body consists of water, and that's why when all the water is stored in a person's leg, something is wrong.

I looked at my neighbor lady next door and knew she didn't have long to live. The shadow she cast was thin. Even when she was home, it was as though she wasn't there. She caught a cold and it became pneumonia. She called at 8:30 one night and wanted me to go buy some orange juice for her. I went and got it. The next day her daughter came and she was gasping for air. They took her to the hospital.

During sickness, the most important thing is mind and spirit. You must have the courage and strength to fight for life. Yamaoka Tesshu, a Meiji Restoration scholar, was told by his doctor that he would die within three weeks. But he said, "You watch," and he lived for another eight years. When he died, he put on a *hakama* [pleated skirt], and *montsuki* [a formal gown with family crest; the two are worn on formal occasions], and with fan in his hand he died sitting up.

Food is life . . . you must think of food as medicine. Natural things are the best. Rather than add salt and seasonings, it is best to eat things in their natural state. That is hard to do because we have a human's mouth . . . but natural foods have their own seasoning.

The worst thing to do is overeat. You shouldn't eat until you are hungry. That is the signal that your stomach has digested its food and is ready for more. In that way a pig is more aware than humans.

I am forever thinking of ways to stay healthy. When I watch television, I roll the balls of my feet over this hard metal ball. It helps keep the liver in good shape. When I feel a cold creeping up, I put an *umeboshi* [pickled plum] in my mouth. It helps kill bacteria. They say if you visit someone with tuberculosis, put an *umeboshi* in your mouth and visit them. Garlic and kelp also ward away colds.

Sickness stems half way from the mind. If you get angry, your blood gets acidic, but if you are happy, your blood is *arukarisei* [nonacidic]. That's why the main problem and concern is how to stay happy. You can't cure just the specific illness: You must cure the entire body through diet, exercise, mind, spirit, and proper behavior.

A human's greeds are many — a conglomeration of desires, lust, and passion. Humans have two polar natures: bad and good, loose and strict. That's why people fast to make their wills stronger. The priests of past times practiced asceticism to cleanse their souls and to make their wills stronger. It is hard to become a good person by one's own strength. That's why we must draw from the strength of *kami-hotoke*[21] [Shinto gods and Buddhas] for they are as different from humans as heaven is from earth.

There are many Buddhas but there is only one true *hotoke* [Buddha] . . . that is Amida Nyorai.[22] In this world the *hotoke* who made the universe is Amida Nyorai. I have read about many religions . . . there are all kinds. Learning about them is like climbing a mountain: There are many different ways to climb it, but at the top is Amida Nyorai. He is like the sun. He has the power to save and sustain all living things. He said that he cannot claim to be a *hotoke* unless he could do that much.

O-shaka-sama [the Sakyamuni Buddha] is the one who revealed

Amida Nyorai as the true Buddha. Hana *matsuri* is the celebration of O-shaka-sama's birthday. On that day you should go to the temple and pour water from a ladle onto a small figure of O-shaka-sama who is pointing to the heavens. He was born from under the armpits of his mother while she was trying to pick a beautiful flower. When he was born, he walked from the moment of birth. From ten years of age, he saw with different eyes. He had compassion for those living in poverty and disease. A fortune teller said he would not only be a savior of his country but also of the world. He married, left his family, and led a life of asceticism in the mountains.

O-shaka-sama fasted and meditated under the bodhi tree so that he could find the happy path for everyone. He sat underneath the tree for three months until he was skin and bones before he was enlightened. It was then that Amida Nyorai was revealed to him as the true Buddha. He is the one who has the power to save everyone in this world . . . all living things. All you have to do is say *Namu Amida Butsu* [invocation of Buddha Amida's name]: This is called *nenbutsu* [a prayer to Buddha]. If you say *Namu Amida Butsu* before you die, he will sweep you into his arms and you will go to *gokuraku* [paradise]. *Gokuraku* is a place where suffering or worries do not exist. If you are hungry, there is plenty to eat . . . if you want to see something, it appears.

Shinran Shonin is the one who founded the Jodo Shinshu sect — the sect I belong to. He made Buddhism much easier to follow. Before, it was difficult. There were many things priests were not allowed to do. They could not eat meat, or fish, and they had to remain celibate. It was too difficult for humans to abide by. Shinran Shonin changed that. He said that as long as you have complete faith in Amida Nyorai and say *Namu Amida Butsu* even once, you will be saved, for within that single, sincere invocation is eternal salvation.

What I want to teach you is a religious way of life. A person who has religion will walk the road of Buddha's teachings: He will find happiness. The moment you are born, you are dying. A husband dies, children grow up, but religion stays with you forever. There are times when you go astray, or times when you are very depressed, so you must greet the day with Hotokesama and *kamisama*.

Death is the greatest event of one's life. But even death is not frightful if you believe in Hotokesama. Hotokesama is just like a parent: he always protects you. His mercy is the same as that of parents for their own child.

This world will become a world of Buddhas if people think of others. But it is human nature to be greedy. It is only when you are a child that you have no greed. As you grow older, greed accumulates and you think only of yourself. That's why you must go to church to hear the right way, to cleanse your soul, to be led on the right path.

It's good to grow old and die because then religion comes over you. When you are young, you don't know what it means to be grateful. When I was younger, I remember telling this lady, Kimura-san, that I don't remember doing anything wrong. She told me you are not *itadaitoru*[23] [enlightened]. I said, "What do you mean? I go to church." I thought she was making fun of me . . . why, she always talked bad about people. She was far from being enlightened. But as I look back now, I know she was right. No people can say they have done no wrong. Just living from day to day, you kill the insects as you walk . . . kill things that are living. To survive, we must realize the sins we accumulate.

To be human is a lonely existence. When you are born, you are alone; when you die, you are alone. That's why you must have religion; then no matter how dark a place, you have someone to turn to. Even if you have parents, one day you leave them. You cannot depend on another person to always be there for you: That's why you must have religion. But just because you have religion, everything is not good. *Kamisama* lets people know about life through suffering. If everything was always good, people would not understand life.

Suffering teaches us many important lessons in life. Even for sickness we must be grateful because it teaches us our limits. A person must collect his suffering each day like a special treasure and think he is lucky because there are so many who are less fortunate than he. Rejoice in suffering because it is then that you begin to understand life.

From the moment of birth you are advancing toward death. Once you die, you get reborn. Those who did good deeds in life return as human beings; those who did bad deeds return as animals — dogs, monkeys. When you do good, you get reborn in a good place. That's why in this life you must plant a good seed.

The happiness you find after death . . . that is religion. When I die, I am going where my mother and father are, and when you die, you will join me. You should not be afraid of death. I'm not afraid because when I die, I will become a *hotoke*. What you do on earth, you will realize in paradise.[24]

A human's sins are deep and for that reason we must borrow the strength from Hotokesama. There is not one person in this world who can claim he has never done a bad deed. We cannot always do good as humans. But Hotokesama says he will take you to *gokuraku* [paradise] just as you are. All you have to do is say *Namu Amida Butsu*. Remember this well . . . *gokuraku* is eternal. You close your eyes and it's a year . . . I'll die first so let's meet again in *gokuraku* . . . please say *Namu Amida Butsu*.

Epilogue

REFLECTIONS ON THE PAST

Reflections on the Past

Mama sat proudly in her usual manner with legs tucked under and hands folded gently on her lap. She rehearsed the answers in Japanese: "The first president of the United States was Jo-ji Wa-shin-ton. July 4, 1776 was the day that America declared independence from Britain; there are 50 states but originally there were 13. Do you know who discovered America? Columbus. In 1492."

She continued to tell me about the Constitution of the United States and the Bill of Rights. This year 1980 was the first time since the passage of the McCarran-Walter Act in 1952, which allowed the Issei to become naturalized citizens, that the test could be passed without speaking English. She was determined to get her citizenship.

"I never plan to return to Japan. My children and grandchildren are all American citizens. I do not belong in Japan. There is nothing for me there." Her facial muscles slowly relaxed as her thoughts drifted back to her homeland. "You saw the fine house Mama came from, didn't you? It was much larger when I lived there. Tell me again about your trip to Japan."

We had covered every detail of my trip before but she never ceased to enjoy hearing of the experience. Each time I repeated some of her favorite stories I also managed to recall yet another untold event: "Never in my life have I been treated so well, Mama.

But the image that stands out so clearly now is the last time I saw Uncle Umetaro. He stood by the gate with lantern in hand, his figure enveloped in the dark. I called out to him, 'Uncle, please live long. I will come back to Japan and we will meet again.' I kept waving until our car turned down the hill toward Tomita Machi, Onī-san and Auntie Itsue looked straight ahead at the road, leaving me with the privacy of the night. We drove in silence.

"Onī-san was the first to talk. 'Tell your Mama that she should come back. Uncle and Auntie are both old. You have now paved the way for everyone in America to come.'

"Auntie chimed in, 'Tell your Mama to come home. She could stay in Tomita.'

"Mama, let's you and I go back and — "

"Stop!" Mama cried. "Please stop. I don't want to hear about Japan any more. I can't go back. Let's just keep that a dream."

A dream. That's what Japan symbolized to her now. And as I sank back into the couch and silenty watched her review the lessons for her Saturday afternoon citizenship classes, it occurred to me that exactly 57 years ago America was the dream: a land of opportunity, an adventure to be experienced, then neatly shelved away in photo albums.

"Don't say I never wanted to go back to Japan," she would remind me. "But with the disgrace of being with a man who gambled and the shame of living such an abject life in America, I never went back." The avoidance of shame because of failure is a reason why many Issei like Mama did not return to their homeland: The Tanakas kept postponing their return so that they could make more money, but being unsuccessful in their attempts they never did go home.

Mama's face would shrivel in anguish when she recalled that a family friend had the audacity to tell her parents about her life in America: "Why did she have to say anything to my parents? I didn't want them to worry about me, to know the kind of life I was living." But Mama's parents already knew of her plight and her mother spent a great deal of time blaming herself for Mama's marriage. "Please don't mention her name anymore!" she would plead after being reminded about her daughter's hardship in America. "I don't want to think about her suffering."

Haruko, Mama's oldest sister, was quick to blame her parents for Mama's life in America: "They were careless," she claimed. "They didn't give much thought or preparation into her marriage with that man. I knew when I first laid eyes on him that he was no good. But he had a way with words and knew how to impress my mother. All my parents were concerned about was how to make more money. They didn't worry too much about their children's happiness."

Takejiro, Mama's youngest brother, contended: "She wanted to go to America. She was curious and wanted to see it. She went to America with Saburo because she liked him — took a shine to him."

Umetaro, the eldest brother, chuckled: "The night that Saburo stayed overnight at our house, Michiko scrubbed her face so hard to make her skin look beautiful that her cheeks got all red and chafed. But I think the real reason why she went to America was because she didn't want to put up with a *shutome-san* [mother-in-law]."

But Mama placed the blame on herself and accepted the decision as her own: "I was an adventurous sort. I always wanted to see America. I just couldn't wait to see it so I married him. My mother pleaded, 'Stay and I will let you have the noodle shop I just purchased.' But I was determined to seek the new world and went against my mother's wishes."

A deep sense of guilt continued to occupy Mama's thoughts: a guilt of not obeying her parents' wishes, of not fulfilling the duties and obligations that she owed as a daughter-in-law, of not being able to take care of her parents until they died, of not achieving success in the eyes of her parents. "I always think now how *oya fukō* (unfilial) I was," she would lament. "I am suffering punishment now because I wasn't good to them. I didn't even send a letter; I didn't even know when my mother died . . . I had given myself up to despair."

The *on* [a fusion of bestowed benefit and incurred debt] that one owes to one's parents is said to be "deeper than the oceans and higher than the mountains," and could never be repaid. In the traditional Japanese family system, the children should demonstrate a lifelong obedience to the wishes of their parents, particularly in the matters of marriage and life goals. But the everyday hardship of survival and the reality of her degraded life in America kept her from writing home to her parents. Life in America meant moving from camp to camp, following the seasonal crops, and doing hard physical labor. Even when she was pregnant, she worked until she could feel the labor pains, then returned to work a month later. She took pride in the fact that she could do work equal to any man: *doryoku,* doing one's best through constant effort, that was most important.

Hard work was also a way for Mama to expiate her guilt and a means to ward off self-blame for unfulfilled obligations. In the traditional Japanese sense, hard work was not only a means to achievement and success, but also a means by which an individual could maintain his/her self-concept as a virtuous person. Working hard and acting in compliance with norms was gratifying because it provided Mama with a way to retain good self-concept despite her "unfilial" deeds.

In the more immediate sense work meant survival — food and shelter for her children. In the past, the family counted heavily on her additional income, and although Papa was recognized as the head of the household, Mama shared equally in the responsibility as provider and protector, a role in which she held great pride. Papa was aware of the importance that she placed on her role and used it to control her behavior: "Don't go to work!" he would threaten. "After the household chores are taken care of, then go to work." Even after his death, she continued her responsibilities as economic provider, taking menial jobs, reporting to work even when she was ill.

After her children were economically able to support themselves, they would try to convince her: "Mama, you don't have to work so hard anymore. Everyone is doing well; we don't need your money. You should take it easy now, enjoy, spend the money on yourself." But she would stubbornly shake her head: "No! As long as my feet hold out, I will work. With the money I earn I could buy things for my children, give money to my grandchildren; I could do things for other people, and I won't be a burden on anybody. Please don't deny me of my pleasure."

Retiring and adjusting to a new life style was a difficult task for a woman who never allowed illness to stop her from finishing a day's work, and who, even in her seventies, could carry several heavy bundles of laundry up and down four flights of stairs. The weekdays were spent either knitting a blanket for one of her children, reading a book on health or religion, or listening to the Japanese radio station, and waiting for her children to come and visit. An occasional trip to Little Tokyo to purchase groceries and chat with friends broke the monotony of her daily routine.

At night, television was her only companion. She would click on the set even though she couldn't understand what was being said: The voices filled the void. Anxiously, she awaited the weekend when she could view the Japanese programs on Channel 22.

Without work, each day meant creating new reasons for her existence or just waiting for the approach of death. "Now I wake up in the morning and I have nothing to look forward to . . . life drags on meaninglessly to the next day."

"Happiness will not come to you unless you repay the debts you owe to others. You must not forget the *on* that you owe to people." This was a theme that Mama repeatedly mentioned for there had been many times since coming to America that she was unable to repay her *on;* preoccupation with *on* surfaced only after leaving her homeland. *On* was something that she didn't think about while she lived in Japan, where many people were socially obligated to her family. But in America, she was often placed in a position of receiving more than she could repay; a deep sense of gratitude to others and the display of humility were her way of coping with her unfulfilled obligations. Her children would impatiently protest: "Why do you have to lower your head so much? Enough is enough!" But Mama's reply was: "How could I lift my face when everyone knows how indebted we are to others? Alone, we can do nothing."

The Issei turned to each other in times of need for support, pooling together money and resources, and in the process of depending upon one another they created an intricate network of social obligations and indebtedness that helped them adjust to their hostile environment. For Mama, turning to others within the ethnic community during times of need was her only logical alternative. Shame inhibited her from writing home to her family for money, and distrust, pride, and fear kept her from turning to the American government for financial assistance.

The Issei in America were "Oriental" immigrants and classified as "aliens ineligible for citizenship." This status stripped them of legal protection and made them targets of effective discriminatory legislation and recipients of all the hostile sentiments directed at the Chinese who had come before them. In 1923, one year before anti-Japanese agitation had reached such a peak that Japanese immigration was virtually stopped, Mama and Papa came to America. The host society defined the limits of their economic and social activities by relegating them to menial labor and segregating them into their own ethnic enclaves. Papa secured the seasonal farm jobs while Mama worked as cook and field hand in either their own or other Japanese-operated labor camps. For Mama, life was even more circumscribed by the additional responsibilities of household chores, childrearing, and the dominance of an overbearing husband.

In Japan, both ideal and law assigned women to a social position far inferior to that of the men: Men made the important decisions and women subordinated their wishes and needs to those of the household. But regardless of the society or time period, a strong-willed, wise, or beautiful woman was not easy to dominate. In Mama's family, her mother made all the important decisions concerning the business. Her astute mind and business acumen was the bargaining power that she had with her husband. Mama recalled, "She could add up 20 items in her head without an abacus. Everything she touched turned to gold and everything Father meddled with became worthless." Other men recognized her capabilities and would come to consult with her about their investments.

But as for Mama, her bargaining position was minimal. She was totally subordinate in her relationship with Papa. If she had remained in Japan, her formal education and her family's social position could have been her bargaining tools. But being in a foreign country, far away from her family ties, confronted with strange ways and new situations, and unfamiliar with the English language, she became even more dependent on a strong-willed man who dominated practically every sphere of family life.

Mama and Papa fought incessantly. She would nag Papa about his gambling, making him even more furious and triggering off another round of arguments. After surviving a barrage of caustic abuse and ridicule, Mama would make excuses for his temper and even manage to laugh. This rankled her children: "How can you laugh! How could you humor Dad after he has treated you like that? How could you even touch him? We can support you. Why don't you leave him!"

Mama would quietly listen, then remark: "You children are young and impetuous. No matter if he drinks or gambles, he is still your father." For despite all the arguments, Mama did have a special love for him. When Papa wasn't gambling, he filled the house with laughter. He had a way of creating excitement and making the mundane seem extraordinary. He turned hard work into a game, everyday cooking into a festivity, rattlesnake meat, spoon turtle, and jackrabbit into delicacies. But that was only when he wasn't gambling.

Papa was addicted. Even if he knew he had to feed thirteen children, he would gamble away the season's earnings and return home with an unlikely story: "Somebody must have noticed me cashing a payroll check. He followed me out of the bank and hit me over the head. In the morning I came to and found myself lying in a vineyard. The money was gone!"

Did Papa gamble because he felt that he had made a mistake by marrying Mama and coming to America? Mama claimed, "He used to remind me that he wanted to marry his brother-in-law's daughter . . . a rare beauty and a geisha, trained and well accomplished in the arts." Was gambling an escape from the responsibilties as father of thirteen children? Or did Papa gamble to cope with the frustrations and loss of pride he experienced in America — a society that had closed its doors to further "undesirable" Japanese immigration and had stripped the ambitious of opportunities and expectations? He realized that there were hardly any Japanese counterparts to the Horatio Alger story such as George Shima, the Issei "Potato King," who created an agricultural empire out of unwanted land. And especially after the passage of the 1913 and 1920 Alien Land Laws, which essentially prohibited the Issei from owning or leasing land, his prospects as a successful farmer were dismal. Maybe by gambling he could make that one "big score" so that he could return to Japan a rich and proud man?

Whatever Papa's reasons were for gambling, his addiction seemed incorrigible. Nevertheless, from his wife and children, he expected and demanded steadfast discipline. His primary concern within the household was to maintain family order and unity and the way he chose to do that was by emphasizing traditional patterns: respect and unquestioned obedience to parents and to elder siblings was the rule that governed the household members. Papa would discipline the children, and even instruct Mama on how to prepare various Japanese foods, how to wear a kimono, how to walk like a refined lady, or how to iron a shirt. The daughters recalled that "Everything we heard, knew, felt, or dreamed of came from within the household." Papa forbade his daughters to date, or to engage in any social activity that did not include the family. Even choice of marriage partners was up to his discretion. He lectured each night during dinner on every subject imaginable while everyone listened in silence. Most of the lectures pertained to some aspect of Japanese traditions, values, or etiquette.

As traditional as Papa was, he must have been disappointed with the birth of ten daughters and only three sons. But he was proud of the way he had raised them and basked in glory when people would say, "If it's Tanaka-san's daughters, you can be sure they'll make good *yome-sans* [daughters-in-law]. Papa continued to dream of the day when the family would return to Japan and his daughters would be great beauties who knew all the proper social graces. Because of his own parentless childhood, drifting from relative to relative, Papa was keenly aware of the importance that formalities, appearances, proper language, and social graces played in the acceptance of an individual.

He would harangue: "Don't be fools! Learn your culture. Now is the only time you are going to get to learn it. Don't be ashamed of it: You should be proud! There'll come a time you will be proud that you know about Japanese culture, that you speak Japanese." He was determined that his children would not be misfits should the family return to his homeland.

But he was also aware of the possibility that his children might never see Japan. Coming to America, living as a minority, and facing racial prejudice and discrimination for the first time, he knew how difficult it would be for his children who had not experienced the security and knowledge of a country where they were of the majority. What he tried to instill in his children was a sense of pride. He knew its importance as long as one remained physically identifiable: "During my lifetime I hope that I can convince you, that as long as you look Japanese, you are going to be Japanese. No one is going to say, 'Oh look, there goes an American.' And you may never see Japan, but everybody is going to say, 'There's that Japanese girl.' "

Emphasizing Japanese traditional patterns and imparting a sense of pride about being Japanese were useful mechanisms to cope with racism, but it also generated a sense of alienation. Keiko believed that "Instilling of Japanese culture and language only brought out the glaring differences between ourselves and Americans," and these differences often made her feel like she did not belong. Conflicts multiplied when Papa would say to his children that Japanese were superior in their morals, values, and intelligence, yet they could see for themselves, in their schools, and community, that America had relegated the Japanese Americans to a second-class status.

One of Papa's favorite lectures at the dinner table concerned physical appearances, which were quite often a point of conflict between him and Mama. Papa was a tall, stately man — quite handsome. Although he had only a few articles of clothing to his name, he took great pride in his appearance and made sure that his shirts were neatly starched and ironed and that his pants held a straight crease down the center of each leg. He carried himself with arrogance, always aware of what he looked like, what impressions he was making on others, and what others were thinking.

He wanted his wife to be flamboyant and gay, but Mama was a very modest woman and certainly couldn't afford to be anything else. What was important to her was not necessarily how well one presented one's physical self, but how pure and selfless one's thoughts and actions were. She was not one to fuss over her hair, apply make-up, or buy clothes that she could ill afford.

Papa would scrutinize her appearance and criticize: "Why don't you put on a little make-up? Wave your hair. Make yourself more attractive!" Her feelings hurt, Mama would reply, "It takes money to buy cosmetics. Why, if I had money to buy cosmetics, I'd get stockings for the kids. If I had money to get a permanent, I'd purchase shoes for the children."

"We all had home-made bonnets fashioned out of the same pattern year after year after year," Keiko recalled. "The kids went without but Mom went with even less. She was the last one to get anything. The only new dress she ever owned in her entire life, and I mean to tell you in her *entire life* . . . was when Chieko got married."

Papa had a flair for style. He could make a secondhand suit look tailor-made for a lord. But Mama would look plain even in the fanciest frock. She was humble when others would have been arrogant, self-effacing when others would have less reason to brag. Unlike Papa, she did not want to put on airs when she herself knew how poor we were. According to Mama, how could she boast about her rich upbringing in Japan when she was leading such an abject life in America?

Proper dress and cleanliness still hold great importance in Japan today as they did during the Meiji period, but "first impressions" were particularly important for the Issei because intimate personal relations with majority-group members were rare. Survival depended upon the way one presented one's self. The right impression meant securing a job, getting ahead, having a second chance, getting one's foot in the door.

Another tool for one's survival kit included the ability to read others — their motives, thoughts and character — and that's what Papa tried to impart to his children. "He always talked about judging people," Yoko remembered. "I think that if we are perceptive, he helped us to build that perception. For instance, if we were talking about some acquaintance that happened to come over to the house, he would say, 'Now look, there are some people who are simple-minded enough to say, "Oh, she is pretty; she had pretty clothes on. She didn't smell bad . . . why, she is just great!' He said that we have to get one step beyond everybody else. How do you do that? By searching for something beyond that initial perception. You don't just accept a person for what he is saying. That is what he taught."

Papa would berate Mama for not being perceptive, but she attributed their differences in awareness to their childhood upbringing: "I used to think, how come I married a person like this? His thinking differed from mine. Me, I listen to someone and believe what they said. Him, he would say, 'Even if they say such a thing to our face, behind our backs they are saying something else.' He would say things like that but it is because he was raised by *tanin* (unrelated persons). His mind was twisted by *tanin*. He grew up looking at the color of their faces, trying to figure out what they were thinking."

Suspicion of the outside world was what Papa taught to his children, but this was as much a product of dealing with a hostile environment in America as it was a product of his upbringing in Japan. For the Issei, the world was a cruel place full of people who were not beyond suspicion. By not accepting things at face value, people were better equipped to protect themselves.

Papa also taught his children to be quiet and observant in situations when one was in doubt of the proper action or behavior; aware of his children's social naivety, he tried to recreate the outside world for them: "This is why I tell you all these things, so that when you leave this house, you are going to know about life as though you have been out in the world. If you should go to a party and there is silverware lined up on the table, what are you going to do? You wait. You sit quietly and just wait for the others to start eating. People will look at you and think that you are just being polite, that you are waiting for the others to begin. They won't realize that you don't know what silverware to use. So what you do is watch others who seem to know what they are doing. If you see a finger bowl come to the table, and you don't know what to do with it, you don't immediately poke your finger in it or start drinking from it. You wait! You just wait."

For Papa, doing the "proper thing" held great importance and approaching new situations with caution meant less risk of mistakes and greater opportunity for making the right impressions and getting ahead of the other person. For Mama "proper behavior" and making the right impressions meant acting in accordance with her status within her own ethnic community and covering her embarrassment by acting humble. The main difference was that Papa had to confront the white man for survival while Mama had only to deal with her family and the Japanese community. Both adapted their behavior to appropriately suit their situation and position within their social environment.

Concealing one's emotions was something that Mama and Papa both practiced and impressed upon their children. Yoko remarked, "If you are terribly upset and you just slapped several of your kids and were screaming at your wife, the minute somebody steps in the house, you turn on a smile . . . see? Because Dad said, it is not necessary for anybody, except for those you want, to know your deepest emotions. And Dad was able to do that. To him, it was important. To me, it made such good sense."

Mama agreed that negative feelings must be concealed before others: "The worst thing to do is show an angry face. You must present a happy face. If something gets you angry to the stomach, or you are very depressed, you should at least recognize another's presence, otherwise you are discourteous. Our Papa said even if you fight to a point where you are both falling out the window, a woman must show a smiling face to other people." Concealing one's real emotional feelings was particularly useful while dealing with the white majority. To show a "good face" as a representative of the Japanese in general insured greater acceptance by the majority society.

Above all, a woman had to hold her man up high in public. Under the surface of Mama's outward submissiveness was a person whom Papa could always count on for inner strength and courage. When the money was all spent from gambling and no prospects of work lay ahead, she was the one that Papa sent out to borrow money. Papa would indulge in his gambling with the security of knowing that Mama would never desert the children and would somehow find a way to provide for them. Several incidents help to illustrate how Papa engaged Mama to do the distasteful or fearful things which he didn't want to face himself.

When the family lived on the Kettleman Ranch, a fire enveloped the bath house at night and threatened to spread to the other buildings. The only source of water was a well, dug 15 feet deep and 30 feet in diameter. The motor to the pump rested at the bottom of the well. "Old woman," commanded Papa. "Go down and start the pump." Mama climbed down the dark pit. Somebody had to do it, but it wasn't going to be Papa.

On another night, while the family lived at the Payne's, a sound was heard coming from the kitchen long after everyone had gone to bed. Mama and Papa lay quietly listening. The noise continued. "Old woman, go see what it is," said Papa, acting like he was too groggy to get up. Mama quicky threw on her robe and ventured out into the dark. The kitchen was located in a separate building approximately 20 feet away from the sleeping quarters. Both buildings were shaded by the huge branches of an oak tree and as she switched on the outside light, its pointy-edged leaves cast eerie shadows on the smooth ground below. Armed only with a flashlight, Mama entered the kitchen. There, next to the cupboards, sat Duchess, the Saint Bernard, slobbering over the bones that Papa had just purchased that day.

Nothing seemed to frighten Mama except when sickness came to her children. She would stay up all night sponging the child's body to lower the fever and boil Vick's vaporizer to ease the breathing of congested lungs. "You're in your glory when the children are sick," Papa would accuse. "Now come to bed!" But the fear of losing her children to sickness and poverty was too real after the death of her two sons, and she would stay awake nursing her child until the morning.

Mama was also the person that Papa could turn to for emotional support. She appreciated his frustrations while dealing with the white society. "A man holds the biggest task of going out to face the world and bringing home the money," she would remark. She recognized his need to feel as though he had control over his environment. At home she would soothe his frustrations and uplift his ego through praise.

"My, you sure can talk," she encouraged when Papa came home from the market after negotiating his crops. "You are really a tough one . . . you really buffaloed them! Show me again how you did it." Papa would oblige without any further encouragement. Turning his back to her to fall into character, he then assumed his "Humphrey Bogart" stance, one of his favorite movie characters.

Mama was someone that Papa could always depend on. She was the one who provided the emotional security for the entire family. While Papa was volatile, unpredictable, and unyielding, Mama was patient, dependable, and forgiving. Just before his death, he would admit to her that "Without you, I could have never made it."

"When dealing with the white man, one must be assertive," Papa would declare. Although he did not allow his children to engage in free verbal communication with him, he stressed its importance in their interactions with others. "He wanted his kids to be the kind of person who, when called upon, can get up and say what needs to be said," Yoko recalled. "He did it. He could be a master of ceremonies at a wedding or could eulogize at funerals. Yet he was a man with no formal education. He would say, 'You should be able to get up, make a speech, sing, do any of these things when you are called upon.' That's the kind of person that he wanted his children to be."

Papa's suppression of free verbal exchange between parent and child, and yet his expectation of assertiveness while dealing with others, was a point of conflict for his children. Outside the household, the children had to force themselves to assume a style that was not comfortably theirs. "At home we were taught to shut up and listen," said Yoko, "but with *hakujin* [whites] we had to speak up loud and clear or never be heard. We had to learn how to switch styles of communication from group to group so that with *nihonjins* [Japanese] we used a more subtle, group-consensus approach, making sure not to be too loud and pushy, and with *hakujins* we used a more aggressive, individualistic approach, putting ourselves out in front so that we could be seen and heard."

The Japanese child was taught implicitly by example the importance of silence and was negatively sanctioned for being too loud and talkative. This was the case in the Tanaka household, where the children were taught not to "talk back," while the American child was encouraged to "speak up." The children were also taught to be extremely sensitive to the social status of the persons with whom they were interacting (higher-lower status, elder-younger, male-female) using the appropriate speech patterns and the proper behavioral patterns for the various statuses.

Since Papa was so strict and demanding, Mama was more lenient and accepting. "It would have been insufferable for my children if I were as strict as Papa," she remarked. She never contradicted Papa, not even in the most subtle manner, for he would cut her down in an instant. Instead, while Papa would discipline his children by lecturing, Mama would teach them through parables.

"Mama had story-telling time and each story had a moral to build one's character," recalled Hana. "Once when Nesan was talking back to Mama, instead of striking or reprimanding her, she told us a story. It was about a little boy who always sassed back to his mother. No matter how much he was disciplined, he continued in the same manner. One day as he was talking back to his mother, lightning struck him and *bachi ga attata* [he was punished by heaven.] We knew that Mama made up the story and it was meant for Nesan."

Whereas Papa emphasized the importance of impressing others through one's manners, speech, and appearance, Mama stressed the goodness of one's heart. Keiko remembered that "Daddy's strategy to success was to be one jump ahead of the other guy, to 'out-fox' him. What you say will impress him. But Mama used to say that if you are good inside, it will show. What Dad said may bring immediate results because you can fool someone who is not too bright, but in the long run, you don't feel too good about yourself. You have to be able to live with yourself and when your mind is wretched, then so is your life."

As long as Papa was alive, he was the undisputed authority within the family. No one dared to disobey him except Naomi. "*Katte ni se!* [Have your own way!] But don't come around again!" he threatened. Naomi had made up her mind to move to San Francisco and put herself through college, yet she was determined to see her family regardless of what Papa said.

"When are you going to give up that nonsense?" Papa would yell.

"Don't you care about your parents? Don't you care about your sisters and brothers? Can't you contribute?" To his other daughters he would denigrate her actions: "She is selfish for pursuing her own personal goals. She's only a fool chasing rainbows."

Afraid of Papa and eager to please him, the sisters openly ridiculed Naomi's mannerisms: "Who does she think she is? Scarlett O'Hara?" But secretly they envied her for her new life style and admired her courage to challenge Papa. On her visits back home, Naomi opened up another world to her sisters which they had envisioned only in the movies. Dressed in brown alligator shoes and lavender gabardine suit, she returned with books and gifts. "There's more to life than just pleasing Dad," she would tell them. Then bundling herself up with long-sleeve shirt, bonnet, and gloves to protect her skin from the sun, she would go out into the fields and help her sisters pick the crops as she told them about life outside the family. "What a story teller she was!" Keiko reminisced. "She would tell us about *Ben Hur, Tale of Two Cities, Les Misérables*. We would beg her to continue and she relished every last bit."

Naomi's decision to move out on her own and put herself through school would have been lauded by an American family as demonstrating initiative and drive, but was considered by Papa as showing willfulness and impropriety. His main concern was to keep the family together and to maintain parental authority. If one daughter was allowed to pursue her own personal goals and go against parental wishes, then the others would also dare to do the same.

Naomi was also the first daughter to set the conditions for her own marriage while Papa was still alive. The other sisters before her had their marriages arranged, but Naomi chose her own husband and proceeded to make plans without the intervention of a *baishakunin* [go-between]. The family finally consented to her marriage, but not without conflict.

Papa tried hard to fight the inevitable process of Americanization, but the values that he taught and emphasized were useful for adapting to the America of that time and place: the place — California, the hub of anti-Japanese sentiment; the time — prior to and shortly after World War II, at the height of racism, suspicion, and segregation between the races, and restriction of civil rights and liberties. According to the children, Papa was the one to be respected, feared, obeyed and pleased. Papa was the "superior" one — smarter, more glib, tall in stature, assertive, arrogant, proud, dominant — more American; Mama was the one to be pitied — weak, humble, self-effacing, nonassertive, submissive, agreeable, easy to please — more foreign. It took many years before her children could view her differently. After raising their own children, they saw that it took strength, not weakness, to persevere in her marriage and stand by Papa's side when all seemed hopeless, to subordinate her personal desires to those of her family, to be humble when a lesser person would brag.

Papa's death marked the beginning of many changes within the family. Kenji became the head of the family and Mama entrusted him with the authority formerly held by Papa. This was in keeping with the traditional Japanese family structure, where after the death of the father the eldest son would take the father's position as head of the household, followed in status by the mother, then the daughters ranked by age. But whereas the daughters obeyed Papa as undisputed head of the household, they could not accept their brother in the same position.

As long as Papa was alive, Mama could rest comfortably with her traditional role: Papa made the decisions and she obeyed. But after his death, new role expectations were thrust upon her by her children, which were often discontinuous or in conflict with the traditional ones; the manner in which she chose to deal with each situation was a source of much anxiety.

The first family conflict that tested Kenji's authority and Mama's new role expectations erupted with Yoko, who was expelled from the family because of her increasing involvement with a man of whom the family disapproved. They argued:

"He's just a common laborer no better than all the seasonal workers who come through our camp!" Although he was well-educated, seasonal workers were often thought to be shiftless and transient people without established family bonds.

"With a scar like that, you don't know how it has disfigured his mind!" The Japanese believed that a person who has a severe physical disfigurement must also suffer from a scarred psyche.

"He's an Okinawan — you can't change that!" The Japanese put

Okinawans on the same level as Koreans. (They are considered second-class citizens.) Marriage to an Okinawan in Liberty's small community translated into possible difficulties for future marriage arrangements among the unmarried daughters.

"If you can't listen, you go!" Kenji demanded, trying to emulate Papa. He slapped down $80 and said: "Get out!" His ultimatum enraged Yoko, especially since she was the main person financially supporting the family in the place of her brother who was living in Los Angeles.

The next day Yoko left her job in midafternoon and went home to pack her suitcase. Rummaging through the dresser for her few belongings, she spotted a picture of herself that Mama had propped up against the lamp. It was Mama's last effort, her way of saying, "Please don't go." She turned the picture face down and continued to pack.

Mama entered the room. "Please change your mind. Stop seeing him and Kenji wouldn't have anything to complain about." She continued to plead with her until the packing was finished; then Mama didn't say any more. Instead, out of frustration, she swatted her on her rear end as she left the room.

"That was the first time that Mama ever hit me. It was no consolation because she still could not understand anything. I moved to L.A. and when I was looking in my bag, she had hidden a picture of herself in my suitcase . . . I'll never forget that feeling . . . I still have it. She was an old lady."

Yoko eventually married the man of whom the family disapproved. Even after the family moved to Los Angeles, her brother continued to forbid her to see them. Her marriage dissolved after 20 years: "He never forgot the bitter feelings aroused by the entire incident," she offered as an explanation for their divorce. The family suffered a great deal of sadness and guilt from the conflict and learned a costly lesson: Strict enforcement of the traditional rules will divide the family and threaten the stability of the household.

Years later, Mama expressed to Yoko the guilt that she continued to bear. She blamed herself for Yoko's divorce, for she believed that if she had been more understanding and supportive of her daughter's decision then the conflict which was to develop in their marriage could have been resolved.

But Mama's life up until the time of the incident with her daughter was dominated and determined by men. She chose the more familiar, traditional path — entrusting authority into the hands of her son — which had its rewards of social and economic security in old age. Her expected female behavior from childhood to adulthood had been conditioned on subservience to the male; the expectation that she would live with her son, who would take care of her in old age, influenced her decision to side with him in the conflict. To revise her behavior, assert her authority, and suddenly assume the role of decision-maker and enforcer within the family, could justify punishment in old age and jeopardize the security that she found in placing family decisions in the hands of the head of the house.

In a subsequent situation with her daughter Hana, Mama chose not to follow traditional role expectations in order to avoid the mistake she had made with Yoko. However, failure to do so was also a source of much internal conflict. Mama admitted that one of the things that she would like to do over again involved her action (or inaction) when her daughter Hana got a divorce. Mama wished that "I could have influenced her enough so that I could have said, 'No! You have to stay married,' and she would have listened." Instead, Mama did not intervene in her daughter's decision. Implicitly she knew that her daughter would follow through with the divorce despite her objections. If she had forcefully intervened, threatening her daughter with expulsion from the family, it could have meant an irreparable schism between mother and daughter.

Later, with Keiko's divorce, Mama found a way to fulfill both new and old role expectations. The following is an account told by Keiko just prior to her divorce:

> I got a call early in the morning from my mother-in-law telling me that Mom was there with Kenji's wife. I was surprised . . . didn't know how they even got there. It must have cost her over $20 in cab fare alone. Got to the house and the air was reeking with incense. As soon as I entered, Mom hit me and told me to quickly go and kneel at

the *obutsudan* [Buddhist altar] and pray. I didn't get mad at her because I understood that this is how she had to act in front of my in-laws to save face. She felt so bad that her daughter was the cause and culprit of all this grief. By the time we returned to my house, Mom was talking sanely. She told me, "Keiko-chan, you know why I had to hit you in front of the in-laws." But she still couldn't understand, just as my in-laws, why I wanted a divorce. For the Issei, the only good reason for a divorce would be if the man was a drunk, a gambler, or if he fooled around with other women. Even then, a woman should do *gaman* [endure, tolerate] and sacrifice her own happiness for the sake of the children.

Mama managed to fulfill old role expectations and to save face by going through the formalities of trying to control her daughter's decision and by openly admonishing her for her "disgraceful" actions; she fulfilled new role expectations by supporting her daughter in her decision despite her own personal objections. Within the process, Mama did not change her values. She stood fast to her belief that a woman should endure regardless of her dissatisfactions and place family and children above all other considerations.

The divorce of several of her daughters continued to bring Mama much unhappiness. She felt responsible to the parents-in-law for the "bad behavior" of her daughters. Her daughter's failure to persevere in their marriages served as a reflection of her own failure to raise them with the "proper values."

"If Papa were still alive, they wouldn't dare talk about divorce," she claimed, "but I've been too lenient on them. They all think they could do it themselves. That's why they got a divorce. Their wills are too strong."

Why did the Tanaka daughters turn out to be such strong-willed women? This was a characteristic that both Mama and Papa abhorred yet unknowingly fostered through their daughters' upbringing and their own behavior. The Tanaka daughters were encouraged to compete among themselves and with men. In the home, competition was a way of life where winning meant receiving the little attention available for each child; in the fields, the women had to work fast, even faster than the male laborers, in order to hold their jobs. Their attitude was, "I'm not going to let anybody beat me!" Although they did work equal to a man, in the household they were assigned a subordinate position. Brother was given preferential treatment by virtue of his sex. Although the daughters accepted that fact as a given, they resented his position in the family.

Mama's low opinion of men also helped to shape their attitudes. "They are like children," she snapped. "Without women they are nothing!" Mama's disappointment in men rested primarily in the fact that they did not live up to their role expectations, starting with her father who slept until eleven o'clock in the morning and left the business decisions up to his wife, who was the brains of the operation; then her own husband, who gambled away everything she had worked for and did not adequately provide the support and protection expected from him; and later her son, who relinquished his duties as household successor.

Although the daughters expressed disdain for the submissiveness that their mother displayed with their father, they followed many of the same patterns in the relationships with their own husbands. They tried hard to win praise and approval, were sensitive to others' feelings, and catered to their men's wants and needs, suppressing their own feelings and desires. Exposure to alternative life styles through school and work infused them with expectations of a more "fulfilling" life. As Keiko stated, "I was always suppressing my own needs and feelings just to please my husband. But why couldn't he be more sensitive to me? Why was I the one who always had to please him? Stepping out of the house and observing other relationships made me realize there was more to life than this. Working and seeing that I could make it on my own gave me the courage to divorce him."

Unlike her daughters, Mama expected little from marriage other than the traditional responsibilities: "I didn't care if he didn't come home for days, as long as he provided for the children." According to Mama, "The most important role for a woman is to marry and raise children. To be happy is to have a good husband (one who goes to work and provides economic support) and fine children." Even if a woman has difficulty with her husband, she should endure the relationship for the sake of the children.

Mama was convinced: "They have taken the wrong path and will pay for it in some form during their lifetime." Individualism was tantamount to selfishness and therefore subject to punishment. Consequently, when Keiko got sick after her divorce, Mama said, "*Kamisama* [the gods] showed her that she took the wrong path by making her sick." By putting her own wishes before her children's, she became ill. In another instance, when Hana's second husband was involved in an automobile accident, Mama attributed it to Hana's "wrong doing" — that is, thinking of herself first instead of her duties and obligations to her children and family.

As a reassurance that she had not completely failed in her efforts to raise "good" daughters, Mama pointed to some of her other daughters as successful examples of "ideal" womanhood, particularly her eldest daughter Nesan. Nesan was more like Mama than perhaps any other daughter in the family. Both were exceptionally strong women who endured under the most unbearable of hardships. Both women lost their husbands at the same time, and both totally subordinated their wishes and needs to those of their children and family. Nesan's self-sacrifice had paid off handsomely, according to Mama, because she had managed to send all of her children to college, thereby insuring their economic security.

Mama's greatest expectations lay with her son. With her daughters, they would marry and become part of another family. But with her son, he would remain to continue the family name. Family pressure and expectations seemed even greater for the eldest son of the Tanakas than it was for most Nisei, for he was the only surviving son in a family with ten daughters. Mama and the sisters often turned to him as their "savior" since Papa was unreliable.

But living up to all the family's expectations proved to be an oppressive task and after many years of unsuccessful attempts, Kenji's responsibilities and duties came to be shared among the sisters. In Mama's disappointment she would conclude: "Who am I to blame when I myself was *oya fukō* [unfilial] to my parents. I am suffering punishment for my unfilial deeds."

Suffering had become a way of life for Mama after coming to America. Her religious conviction that "we must count our sufferings as jewels of wisdom" stemmed from the Buddhist belief that "the harsher the winter, the fresher the spring," and helped her to overcome life's obstacles. "Even sickness," she said, "we must be grateful for. It teaches us our limits." She recognized suffering as a learning process . . . a way of understanding and improving life.

Fatalism helped her to accept life's events and conditions. According to Mama, one can look to improve or change one's fate through one's thoughts and actions, but much of one's destiny is set before birth. She believed that, "If you did well in your past life, then it will continue into the next. Just as there are some people who are born into wealth, there are those who can barely eat — it is their past life condition that determines their present." Therefore, the hardships she faced after coming to America, the death of her two sons, the illnesses experienced by her daughters, were events which she accepted as determined by fate: "Within this world it doesn't go as you want . . . it's all determined by fate. That is what they say in Buddhism . . . that is what Issei all believed."

Mama now lives alone. Several of her daughters and even her son have made arrangements for her to live with them but she feels reluctant to accept their offer: she doesn't want to be a burden. Instead, she pursues her daily routine by devoting scrupulous attention to achieving harmony and balance with proper nutrition, exercise, and religion.

My trip to Japan had brought us even closer together. It was a validation of her past: "Yes, Mama, you did come from a fine house." America was a rite of passage from youth, innocence, and the protection of home to adulthood, suffering, and understanding of life. The Issei woman's life in America centered around the family and hard work, and Mama's life history was a testimony to that experience. It was their spirit to do *gaman* [endure], their resiliency and their determination to overcome obstacles, that helped them to persevere at all costs despite their longings and hardships. That the concentration-camp experience was recalled as a happy, carefree time without the worry of supporting her children only helps to illustrate life's adversities for the Issei woman in America.

Mama bustled to the kitchen and busily started to prepare the meal. Eating together had a special meaning for us. Sharing food was her way of showing love and my way of learning more about her past. It was a time for her to teach me the "important lessons in life" and in the process, I was made an "insider" to her world.

We had shared meals together at least once a week for the past five years while I listened and recorded her life history. Mama usually started off each meal by discussing the nutritional value of each ingredient. But that day, passing the citizenship test was foremost in her mind.

"Ask me anything about America," she challenged. Without waiting for me to ask a question, she continued. "Do you know what the colors of the flag stand for?"

She smiled. She knew she had me stumped. "Red stands for courage, white for truth, and blue for justice. I can't speak English very well, but does that make me less of a citizen?"

"Why do you want to become an American citizen?" I pressed. She looked at me as though I had asked a stupid question.

"I have to protect myself," she replied matter-of-factly. "America will be facing hard times. They won't be helping foreigners. I've been here since 1923 — 57 years! I have 11 children . . . 22 grandchildren. All American citizens! I should be entitled to citizenship, but I'm still considered a foreigner."

On May 15, 1980, Michiko Tanaka became an American citizen.

Notes

1. *Tanabata matsuri* [July 7 festival]. The alpha star in the Aquila (Altair) and the alpha star in the Lyra (Vega) are called *Kengyu-sai* [Cowherd Star] and *Shokujo-sai* [Weaving Woman Star] in oriental (Chinese and Japanese) astronomy (and astrology). The Cowherd and the Weaver are separated by the Amanogawa [Heavenly River or Milky Way] between them. They are allowed to see each other only once a year when the Cowherd swims across the river to be with his lover on the night of July 7. The Tanabata Festival was originally to celebrate the reunion of the lovers — the folk story that came to Japan from China. People decorated bamboo trees with colorful paper strips and also with pieces of paper with calligraphy (poems of love and the life). A tradition developed that those who celebrate the Tanabata will make improvements in weaving and sewing because the Weaving Woman in the sky will help. Also those who write poems on pieces of paper to decorate the bamboos will improve their skill in calligraphy (it is not clear why).

2. *Old education system in Japan.* See page 110 for chart.

3. *Shinran Shonin* (1173–1262) is regarded as the founder of the most important of all Pure Land sects, or more simply the True sect (Shinshu). This sect came to be the largest traditional Buddhist group within Japan. Members of Shinran's True Pure Land sect

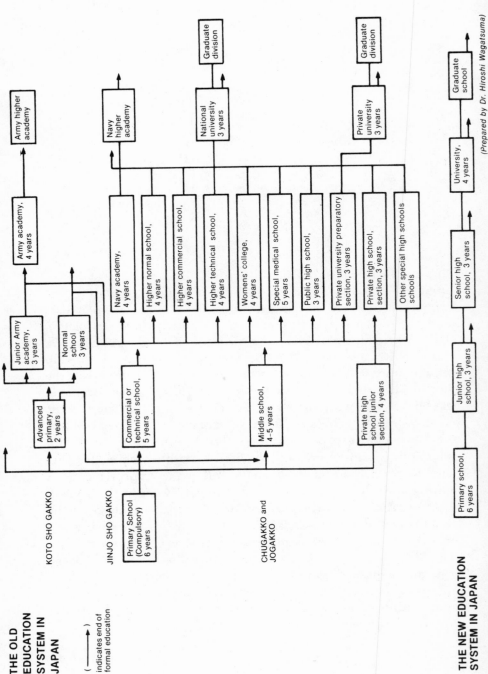

THE OLD EDUCATION SYSTEM IN JAPAN

(———➤) indicates end of formal education

KOTO SHO GAKKO

JINJO SHO GAKKO

CHUGAKKO and JOGAKKO

Army higher academy

Navy higher academy

Graduate division

National university 3 years

Graduate division

Private university 3 years

Army academy, 4 years

Navy academy, 4 years

Higher normal school, 4 years

Higher commercial school, 4 years

Higher technical school, 4 years

Womens' college, 4 years

Special medical school, 5 years

Public high school, 3 years

Private university preparatory section, 3 years

Private high school, section, 3 years

Other special high schools schools

Junior Army academy, 3 years

Normal school 3 years

Advanced primary, 2 years

Commercial or technical school, 5 years

Middle school, 4–5 years

Private high school junior section, 4 years

Primary School (Compulsory) 6 years

THE NEW EDUCATION SYSTEM IN JAPAN

Primary school, 6 years

Junior high school, 3 years

Senior high school, 3 years

University, 4 years

Graduate school

(Prepared by Dr. Hiroshi Wagatsuma)

identified themselves as closely as possible with the ordinary man. Shinran emphasized that exclusive reliance on the power of Amida alone assured direct rebirth in the Land of Bliss. He permitted his priests to marry, a custom which spread to most types of clergy in all sects, in an effort to bring the clergy closer to the people and nearer to everyday life.

4. *Machi geisha.* A geisha is a female who is professionally trained in the art of entertainment: singing, dancing, and playing the *shamisen* [a Japanese banjo]. Papa's youngest sister, Sachiko, was a *machi geisha* who entertained at weddings and parties held in the city of Hiroshima.

5. Michiko refers to Saburo as Papa throughout rest of the text. In the Japanese language, a husband and wife, after becoming the parents of a child, use "Mother" (for wife) and "Father" (for husband) as terms of reference and address. In the English language, a husband talking to his child may often refer to his wife as "mother." For example, he might say, "Go and tell your mother (or Mother) that I am waiting outside." In Japan the same happens except more frequently and consistently. Also very often a husband addresses his own wife as "Mother" and a wife calls her husband "Father."

6. *Hinekureta.* Japanese frequently use the word *amaeru,* which cannot be translated into a single word in Western languages. It means to presume upon other people's love and acceptance. The need to be loved remains ego-syntonic in the mind of adult Japanese, whereas such a need is allowed only for children in the Western culture and therefore has to be repressed as an individual grows up in the Western cultures. Japanese call the behavior of a person whose need for *amaeru* is frustrated by the terms *suneru* [to pretend not to need to be loved] and *higamu* [to pretend not to need to be loved but also to assume that while the person is not loved all other people are loved]. When the *higamu* behavior becomes chronic and a part of one's character traits, such a character trait is called *hine-kureta* [warped, twisted]. Japanese highly value a character trait called *sunao-na* [upright and compliant], which is the direct opposite of *hinekureta.* A *sunao-na* person is one who has enjoyed the gratification of his need to be loved since his childhood and therefore

is basically trusting and obedient and is considered an ideal person in the Japanese culture. The opposite type, the *hinekureta* person, is not pitied but not welcomed.

7. *Burakumin,* or people of special or unliberated communities, is the common term used for Eta, which means outcaste, or literally full of filth. Eta is a pejorative term, as is *yotsu* [four-legged], which implies the subhuman attributes of this outcaste group. During the Tokugawa period (1603–1868) and prior to 1871, this status term was officially recognized in government documents. The Eta and Hinin (literally, nonpeople) were the lowest classes during the Tokugawa period (see DeVos and Wagatsuma, 1966).

8. During the early part of Japanese immigration, it was the Japanese male who predominantly immigrated, sending for his wife several decades later. Female immigration began at the turn of the century and in 1900 there were approximately 24 males in the United States for every female (985 females; 24,326 males). In 1910 there were 9,087 females, and by 1920 there were 22,193 females and 87,817 males. (See Gee, 1971.)

9. In California agriculture, labor camps were established to house the migratory labor force organized by labor contractors. (See "History of Contract Labor in California Agriculture," in Fisher, 1953, pp. 20–41.)

10. This is the second time Michiko describes somebody as "Buddha." There is an old expression in Japanese: "*hotoke-sama no yō na hito* [a person just like Buddha]" for a person who is compassionate, generous, calm, never losing a sympathetic smile, therefore living up to the Japanese ideal: The person was like a Buddha.

11. As the Japanese male immigrants' stay in America became longer than they had intended, many resorted to having their marriages arranged for them in Japan by a go-between rather than making the return voyage, which was quite expensive. These marriages came to be known as "picture-bride marriages"; in essence they were an extension of legal and social customs of Japan. Since the time when photography was introduced in Japan, the exchange of photographs of prospective spouses was a customary first step in the process of arranged marriages that were aided by

go-betweens. The actual physical presence of either spouse was not a necessary legal procedure in marriage. Legal status was acquired after the bride's name was placed in the family registry. However, in response to the exclusionists in America, who condemned picture-bride marriages as an immoral practice, the Japanese government stopped issuing passports to picture brides on February 29, 1921, thus forcing a large number of men to remain bachelors. (See Ichihashi, 1932.)

12. The Immigration Act of 1924, which excluded all aliens ineligible for citizenship, was directly aimed at the Japanese and was the culmination of an organized anti-Japanese movement. (See Ichihashi, 1932, p. 132.)

13. *Bachi ga ataru* [punishment has been inflicted upon a person — *bachi* being the corruption of *batsu* or punishment] is very frequently used in Japanese conversation. Behind the expression is what was originally a Buddhist idea of *inga ō hō* or the law of rewards in accordance with deeds: What one has sown, one will reap. In the notion of karma in Hinduism and Buddhism, one's good or bad deeds in this incarnation bring about the reward or punishment in one's next incarnation. This notion was developed into the ideal that even within this incarnation, one's deed brings its consequences upon one: a reward for a good deed, a punishment for a bad deed.

14. The War Department's decision to recruit and enlist for a special combat team those Japanese Americans who were interned in concentration camps during World War II was accompanied by a decision to register at the same time the entire evacuee population. One of the main sources of debate and anger revolving around those decisions was the questionnaire that all center residents over seventeen were required to answer, regardless of sex or nationality. The most controversial questions were numbers 27 and 28, originally directed at Nisei men of military age. Question 27 asked, "Are you willing to serve in the armed forces of the United States on combat duty, wherever ordered?" Question 28 asked those Nisei men eligible for service, "Will you swear unqualified allegiance to the United States of America and faithfully defend the United States from any

or all attack by foreign or domestic sources, and forswear any form of allegiance or obedience to the Japanese emperor, or any foreign government, power, or organization?"

The compulsory registration, from which only those who applied for repatriation to Japan were exempt, posed the greatest dilemma for the Issei, for a "Yes" answer meant that they would be relinquishing their Japanese citizenship and, since they were not allowed American citizenship, would be stateless. Therefore, a victorious Japan could plausibly have punished them for their disloyalty. Some Issei feared that a "Yes — Yes" response would force them to leave the centers whether they liked or not. Question 28 was later changed for the Issei to read, "Will you swear to abide by the laws of the United States and to take no action which would in any way interfere with the war effort of the United States?" But despite the change, much confusion had already been caused.

The questionnaire created a criterion and impetus for segregating disparate elements. Those whose loyalty to the United States was questionable or whose "disloyalty" was known were placed in Tule Lake center. (For further analysis, see Daniels, 1972; Girdner and Loftis, 1970).

15. *Toyotomi Hideyoshi* (1536–1598) was a man of lowly birth who, preceded by Oda Nobunaga and followed by Tokugawa Ieyasu, restored political unity in Japan, which had been divided by over a hundred years of incessant civil war among approximately 60 independent domains. He unsuccessfully sought to subjugate China and in the process invaded the Korean peninsula in 1592.

16. The Tokugawa Shogunate, starting with Tokugawa Ieyasu, lasted for two and a half centuries (1603–1868). The goal of political peace and stability was secured by rigid controls over society, isolation from the rest of the world, and preservation of many feudal institutions and attitudes of the late sixteenth century.

17. Takasugi Shinsaku (1839–1867) was a leading politican at the end of the Tokugawa Shogunate. He organized a Western-style army, Kiheitai, to overthrow the shogunate. However, before he could witness the Meiji Restoration in 1868, he died of tuberculosis.

18. Itō Hirobumi (1841–1909) took charge of accomplishing the aims of the reforms undertaken in Meiji Japan: to win the respect of

the Western nations and to redeem the humiliation suffered by the forcible opening of the country. He did this in several ways: First, by drafting a constitution; second, by demonstrating Japan's new military strength in the Sino-Japanese War of 1894; and third, by winning revision of the unequal treaties imposed upon Japan only a few decades before.

19. Japanese call the dead *hotoke,* the same word used for Buddha.

20. The Japanese had long discriminated against Koreans, who were colonized by Japanese from 1910 to 1945. They constitute a minority group in present-day Japan.

21. Both Shinto and Buddhism are pantheistic religions and Japanese have believed in both since the introduction of the latter in the fifth century A.D. With an exception of the Imperial family and Shinto priests, most Japanese observe Buddhist funeral ceremonies and ancestor worship services, but practice Shinto rituals for childbirth, weddings, and on numerous other festive occasions. Therefore, when Michiko mentions *kami-hotoke* [Shinto gods and Buddhas] she is simply referring to all the supernatural powers and deities she believes in.

22. Amida Nyorai, Amitābhā Tathāgata, was one of the Buddhist saints who decided to postpone his own salvation (or enlightment) until every human soul was saved. According to Jodo and Jodo Shin sects, the only way for all the humans to attain salvation is to trust and rely on the Amida Buddha's help and benevolence. The Jodo and Jodo Shin sects were founded in Japan by Honen and Shinran in the thirteenth century. Michiko is a follower of the Jodo (or Jodo Shin) sect, the most prevalent one among the Japanese Americans, and therefore she says that the Amida is the only true Buddha.

23. *Itadaitoru,* or to humbly receive, means that one continuously feels grateful to life, to others, and to Buddha, with the thought that all one has and all one is is what has been given to one. Originally, *itadaku* meant to put on one's head, *itadaki* originally meaning the top.

24. Like many Western Christians, the Japanese are often confused about what happens to their souls after their death.

Michiko is confused too. The idea of paradise should be coupled with that of hell. Those who live virtuously go and rest in paradise, while those who do wrong are sent to hell to be eternally punished. This reward and punishment idea is basically incompatible with the idea of *samsara* or transmigration of souls because, according to this idea, a soul does not rest in paradise but has to be reborn and rereborn eternally in the cycle of karma. The enlightenment in Buddhism originally meant freedom from this chain of karma. The idea of transmigration also implies reward and punishment because one who has lived virtuously will be reborn as a better person in a better place, while one who has done wrong may be reborn as an animal in the following incarnation. Michiko does not talk about Hell because she believes she does not have to think about it.

Appendices

The Japanese American Family in Process of Acculturation

Starting from the 1890s Japanese immigrants came to America in larger numbers. Many came with the intention of staying for but a few years and making enough money to settle back in their homeland. The young men came first, settling mainly along the Pacific Coast. The majority of available jobs were found in domestic services and farm labor. But others found opportunity in contract gardening, canneries, railroad construction, lumber mills, mining, logging camps, fishing, and the like, and in small ethnic-oriented businesses like restaurants, hotels, markets, and barber shops.

As hopes or desire of returning to their homeland faded, those men who had wives waiting sent for them while others made the trip home to secure wives. But since this method was too costly, the majority who wished to remain and start families made arrangements back in Japan for "picture brides." This process was done through an exchange of pictures of potential spouses. Scrupulous care was taken by the go-between, who checked the personal characteristics and family background of each party. This practice, which was essentially an extension of social custom in Japan and

119

recognized by Japanese law, was seized upon as immoral by the exclusionists and the practice was terminated after 1921 (Ichihashi, 1969).

Other racial obstacles riddled the lives of the Issei in their new country. The California Alien Land Laws of 1913 and 1920 limited, then prohibited the Issei from owning or leasing land as part of an effort to drive the Japanese out of agriculture (Ichihashi, 1969). Moreover, the Issei were prevented from obtaining United States citizenship, without which one could not even be a tenant farmer. Many put their land holdings under the nominal ownership of their children but the legal difficulties were abundant.

By 1924, the exclusionists were successful in their attempts to stop the flow of Japanese immigration. With the suspension of Chinese immigration already accomplished by the Exclusion Act of 1882, the Immigration Act of 1924, excluding "aliens ineligible to citizenship," effectively singled out the Japanese for exclusion from the United States.

Within the Japanese population emphasis shifted from the immigrant to the American-born generation, the Nisei, the majority of whom were born between 1910 and 1930. Within this generation rested the hopes and dreams of the community for, unlike their parents, they were United States citizens by birth.

However, this status proved to be of little significance with the advent of World War II, as anti-Japanese agitation and mounting racial tension exploded with the Japanese attack on Pearl Harbor. All the racial fears, antagonism, and distrust culminated in an order from the President of the United States, which was stamped with legal approval by the United States Supreme Court and supported by public sentiment, to evacuate more than 110,000 Japanese, aliens and citizens alike, from the West Coast and to concentrate them into camps located in the interior on desolate government land (see tenBroek, Barnhart, and Matson, 1968.)

Today, in spite of their initial harsh encounters of racial, economic, social, and educational barriers, the Japanese Americans have come quite far. Scholars point out that one of the amazing aspects of their acculturation is the speed with which they achieved it (Broom and Kitsuse, 1955; Caudill, 1952; De Vos, 1951; Kitano,

1976). Some attribute this feat to similar emphasis placed on formal education by both American and Japanese cultures and the general accessibility to formal education of Japanese in America (Broom and Kitsuse, 1955). Others have pointed to the compatibility of the Japanese culture and the value system of the American middle class in such matters as sharing common values of politeness, diligence, emphasis on long-term goals, respect for authority and parental wishes, the importance of keeping up appearances. Others note the utilizing of similar adaptive mechanisms, such as being extremely sensitive to cues from the external world and adjusting behavior accordingly, and suppression of desires and real emotional feelings (Caudill, 1952).

The wartime evacuation and concentration have also been pointed out as one of the most influential factors in the Japanese American's speedy acculturation (Kitano, 1976). Their incarceration broke up the communities in which the Japanese were previously concentrated, dissolved old institutions and structures (such as business establishments, Japanese associations, churches, and Japanese language schools), divided community members into separate factions, stripped them of their land and possessions, weakened and reordered the family structure, broadened generational differences, and separated and scattered family members into different parts of the country that formerly had no Japanese population. The push to prove themselves loyal American citizens led many in the younger generations of Japanese Americans to deny their ancestral heritage.

However, one of the most influential factors contributing to the Japanese American's rapid accomplishments — in high education, in upward economic and social mobility, and in low record of social deviance (crime, delinquency, and mental illness) — is the Japanese family and its approach to socialization and social control, its values and norms, and its role in integrating the conflicting demands of Japanese and American life styles (Caudill, 1952; Kitano, 1976; Petersen, 1971).

To better understand the Japanese Americans and their present family structure and the cultural continuities and discontinuities from Japan, it will be useful to look briefly at the pre-War Japanese family system and the social structure in which the Issei were reared.

TRADITIONAL JAPANESE SOCIETY
AND FAMILY

The Issei, for the most part, were of the first generation to be born after the Tokugawa feudal era, which had lasted from 1603 to 1868. Even in the wake of rapid industrialization and a conscious effort toward modernization, many of the old traditions and values were tenaciously preserved. It was these old customs and patterns of social behavior developed over approximately 300 years of Japan's feudal period that the Issei tried to impart to their children, the Nisei.

Feudal Japan

During the long period of Tokugawa feudalism a rigid hierarchical social system had developed, similar to a caste system based on hereditary and occupational endowment. Society was divided into three classes: The first was the ruling class — the warriors and administrators; the second was the ruled class, which included farmers (independent and tenant), artisans, and merchants; the third was the outcastes — the Eta (pollution abundant) and Hinin ("nonhuman"). This outcaste class engaged in what was considered the most lowly occupations: begging, entertainment, working for the police as prison guards and executioners, and making leather goods (in the Shinto religion, contact with anything dealing with death or blood was polluting) (see DeVos and Wagatsuma, 1966.) This long period of feudalism conditioned by a rigid class stratification resulted in "the general disposition to accept authority, formalization of status, glorification of military values and codes of the 'samurai' (warriors), collectivity-orientation, and an extreme 'other-directed' definition of situations" (Iga, 1957:274).

The social values crystallized during this period were very important for the moral foundation of modern Japan. With the Meiji government's decision to readopt Confucian values as the foundation of moral education, implemented through universal education, these values came to permeate down to the lowest stratum of the Japanese population, whereas until 1868 they had been more or less limited to the samurai class (and upper-class farmers and merchants). Therefore, in spite of institutional and legal changes entrained by industrialization and westernization, behavioral patterns and psychological attitudes of this period continued to persist.

The backbone of this period was Confucian ethics, which emphasized duty, obedience, filial piety, ancestor worship, and *bushido* — the way of the warrior, which began in the fourteenth century and stressed *giri* (indebtedness). Codes of appropriate behavior in interpersonal relationships were rigidly prescribed according to role-status, age, and sex. Specific behavior was required between lord and subject, father and son, husband and wife, older and younger sibs, and friends and friends. The ultimate importance in a relationship was knowing one's role in relation to others and thereby fulfilling the appropriate obligation, duty, and loyalty owed to others in each situation. Adherence to the required behavior was a sign of virtue.

The importance of status and role consciousness was also built into the Japanese language itself, which has specific ways of addressing others depending on the role-status of the individuals. As Ruth Benedict observed, there was great security to be found by the individual in knowing precisely how one should behave in any given situation:

> If the Japanese loved and trusted their meticulously explicit map of behavior, they had a certain justification. It guaranteed security so long as one followed the rules; it allowed protests against unauthorized aggressions and it could be manipulated to one's advantage. It required the fulfillment of reciprocal obligations. (Benedict, 1946:73-74).

The Traditional Family System

The traditional family system was a conceptualized set of behavioral patterns and standards against which actual conduct was measured; deviations from these prescribed standards were socially disapproved (Dore, 1958). It was a norm by which the Japanese

family guided their behavior but it was not necessarily representative of what people actually did. The following description of the
family system illustrates what the Japanese family thought they
should do prior to World War II (see Wagatsuma, 1977).

Central to the concept of the Japanese family system was the *ie*
[family, household, house], the primary unit of social organization.
As a legal and political organization it was based upon Confucian
political principles, which generally stated that stable families
insured a stable society. The *ie* was an entity continuous through
time, including all past, present, and future members of the family,
and was of greater importance than any of its members and their
individual interests and goals. It was a composite of concrete and
abstract, material as well as spiritual elements — the family name,
occupation, property, tradition, family altar, graveyard, and the
family code that listed expected behavior.

Since continuation of the *ie* was of utmost importance to the
family's future, marriage and the selection of prospective mates
was a serious matter that concerned the entire family. The social,
psychological, and physical backgrounds of the prospective mates
and their families were carefully scrutinized before arrangements
actually proceeded. Marriages were made for the purpose of produc-
ing an heir; marriage for the sake of love was considered immoral
because it was an assertion of individual interest and welfare above
that of the *ie*. Continuation of the *ie* was so important that adoption
(of a daughter, husband, or husband and wife) was practiced when
there were no offspring to insure its perpetuity. In cases where a wife
was unable to bear children, it was not unusual for the husband to
find a mistress to bear his child without replacing his wife.

The moral as well as legal duty of continuing the *ie* was vested in
the househead *[kachō]* who, as eldest son and heir to the property
rights, had the obligation of securing a stable environment for its
members and of providing arrangements for marriage, occupation,
food, and living comforts. His authority emcompassed final decisions in matters concerning marriage, choice of occupation, place of
residency, and expulsion from the family, for each member of the
ie. However, his authority was to be enforced not for personal
whimsy but for the good of the *ie*.

Dedication of one's life for the advancement and good reputation of the *ie* was an obligation not only observed by the househead but also by each of its members. Respect, obedience, and filial piety to parents and ancestors (especially toward father) was highly empha- sized along with observance of rank order within the family structure. Generally, respect was required from persons of lower rank to a person of higher rank: from younger member to older member, from children to parents, from wife to husband.

THE JAPANESE AMERICAN FAMILY

Attempts to preserve the *ie* ideal have continued to persist within the Japanese American family (Connors, 1974b), but it has been modified to suit the new country and situation. The Issei came alone and did not have their parents and extended family to whom they had to pay their obligations, duties, and responsibilities. Instead the *ie* was adapted to encompass a larger unit — the village or *ken* [district] from which they came, or the entire Japanese community itself. The larger unit functioned similarly to the *ie*, serving as an effective device for social control (Kitano, 1976).

Individual interest was subordinated to that of the community with the understanding that what an individual did (good or bad) would cast a reflection not only upon one's self and one's family, but also upon the entire community. The major concern was showing a "good face" to the *hakujin* (Caucasian). Community solidarity was high when it came to dealing with the majority group. Individuals were encouraged and often socially pressured into behaving in a way that would benefit the reputation of the family and all Japanese. The Japanese community in turn furnished the security that rested in the *ie* in Japan, providing a sanctuary from the often hostile majority group. Ethnic businesses and services such as restaurants, markets, and Japanese-language schools flourished, providing employment, socialization opportunities, and recreation.

Since World War II the demographic concentration of Japanese within their own communities is considerably less. There are several reasons for this. First, the War and the ensuing concentration of Japanese into camps scattered many families throughout different parts of the country after its end. Second, their rising socioeconomic status and their educational and occupational mobility enabled them to move into areas that they had never entered before. Third, better facility with the English language, familiarity with American ways of life, and less overt racism and discrimination allowed for greater interaction with the majority group. Nevertheless, especially in California and Hawaii where the largest concentration of Japanese Americans exists, in-group association remains high. Japanese American athletic teams, community organizations, and clubs are still abundant.

Current Studies on the Japanese American Family

Levine and Montero (1973) have suggested that within the Japanese American community there flow two different streams (in both of which the Nisei's children, the Sansei generation, navigate): one more traditional, and the other more assimilationist. They predicted that if the Sansei's high educational training and skills and their emphasis on socioeconomic success disperse them geographically into a widely scattered minority, then radical changes such as the destruction of the more Japanese overtones of Japanese America could be expected.

Current research on the Japanese American family suggests that despite the social mobility and acculturation of each successive generation, family solidarity and certain Japanese values continue to exist. Connor's study (1974b) of three generations of Japanese Americans in Sacramento provided evidence that despite the acculturation of each successive generation, the importance of family and the inculcation of group dependency needs persisted. Johnson's study (1977) of Japanese American kinship relations in Honolulu revealed a persistence and even an increase in kin solidarity and sociability among the Sansei despite their social mobility and increased assimilation into extrafamilial institutions. This was made possible through the process of exchange based upon the traditional Japanese value system of sociocentricity, obligation to parents, reciprocity, and group dependence.

However, she found that within the Japanese American family, structural changes had occurred that tended toward the American bilateral system. Among the Nisei parents and their Sansei offspring, the traditional rule of primogeniture had changed to equal inheritance, which introduced more symmetry into sibling relationships. Obligation to parents was less burdensome and more easy to fulfill since the responsibility toward aged parents was shared by the entire sibling group rather than being the province of the eldest son. Sharing of filial responsibility and more symmetry in the sibling relationships actually increased kin solidarity.

Yanagisako's (1975) analytical distinction between the behavioral and ideational structures of kinship, in her study of changes in Japanese American kinship, helps to elucidate Johnson's findings. Yanagisako demonstrated that social-structural changes in kinship can occur without changes in the cultural structure of kinship (referring to the system of symbols and meanings embedded in the normative system). That is, social structural changes may occur without accompanying modification in the symbolic structure itself or in the underlying traditional values. Therefore, in reference to Johnson's study (1977), equal inheritance and symmetry in sibling relationships can occur within the kinship structure without accompanying modification in the traditional Japanese value system of sociocentricity, obligation to parents, reciprocity, and dependence.

Yanagisako (1977) also recognized the central role of the female in promoting household solidarity. She found that pairs of female kin (mother-daughter and sister-sister) had more frequent contact and affective solidarity with their primary kin (parents, children, and siblings) than pairs of male kin (father-son and brother-brother). Women maintained closer ties through telephoning, letter writing, and visiting each other than the males; women made the arrangements and plans for family events and holiday gatherings. Whereas in the traditional Japanese family the female was presumed to have left her natal family at marriage to become a part of her husband's family, in the Seattle Japanese American family, the man was said to be the one who was lost by joining his wife's family.

Current studies on the Japanese American family indicate the process of acculturation is not a linear phenomenon, so that despite culture change, the feelings of family solidarity and the retention of certain Japanese values still persist and in some cases increase. The elements of both cultural change and cultural persistence within the Japanese American family should be the target of further research.

Socialization

Caudill and Weinstein (1974) note in their study on maternal care and infant behavior in Japan and America that the two cultures practice different styles of caretaking and that by three to four months of age the infant in both cultures becomes habituated to respond appropriately to its style of caretaking.

A follow-up study by Caudill and Schooler (1973) of the same sample of children and caretakers at different ages (two and a half years old and six years old), demonstrated that the essential cross-cultural differences in behavior in the three- to four-months-old infants were repeated at age two and a half and again at age six.

Caudill and Weinstein (1974) suggest that the basic difference in behavior is that in Japan "there is an emphasis on interdependence and reliance on others, while in America the emphasis is on independence and self-assertion" (p. 229). First, the Japanese are group-oriented and interdependent compared to the Americans, who are more individual-oriented and independent. Second, the Japanese are more self-effacing and passive while the Americans seem more self-assertive and aggressive. Third, the Japanese rely more on emotional feeling and intuition in matters that require a decision, in contrast to the Americans, who emphasize rational reasons for their actions. Fourth, the Japanese use more forms of silent, nonverbal communication in interpersonal relations—gestures and physical proximity—in contrast to the Americans, who predominately rely on verbal communication.

Caudill and Frost (1974) did a comparable study of everyday behavior with Japanese American mothers and their three- to four-months-old infants to determine whether behavioral differences are due more to genetic factors or to cultural learning or to conditioning and to determine whether significant shifts in infant behavior will occur as succeeding generations of mothers care for their infants in a different style within the context of social change. Their findings indicate that Japanese American mothers and infants are closer in their styles of behavior to the American than to their Japanese counterparts. The Sansei mother is more like the American mother than the Japanese mother in certain respects. First, she engages in greater amount of chatting to her baby than the Japanese mother. Second, she does more positioning and less rocking than the Japanese mother. The Yonsei baby (fourth generation) is more like the American baby than the Japanese baby in that he engages in greater amounts of happy vocalization and physical activity and lesser amounts of unhappy vocalization.

However, that the influence of cultural persistence is still operational is also demonstrated. Results indicate that the Sansei mother is more like her Japanese counterpart than the American mother in certain other respects. First, she does more carrying of her infant and more lulling than the American mother. Second, she spends a greater amount of time playing with her infant than the American mother. Related to this finding is that like the Japanese baby, the Yonsei baby spends less time playing by himself than does the American baby.

There is other evidence to support the assumption that differing emphases in family life and interpersonal relations still continue to exist among the Japanese Americans. Johnson (1977) found interdependence expressed in various areas of Japanese American family life in Hawaii. First, young people are expected to live with the family until marriage. Second, aged parents live with a member of the family rather than in a nursing or old-age home. Third, all age levels are usually integrated into family and kin activities rather than age-segregated social networks.

Connor's results of the Edwards Personal Preference Schedule (EPPS) (1974a) showed that when compared with a Caucasian student sample, the Sansei consistently scored higher on those variables that indicate retention of values associated with the traditional Japanese family, especially those indicating dependency needs.

Iga (1957) also found significant differences between Japanese Americans and Caucasians among the following variables: conformity, compromise, success, aspiration, obligation and dependency. The Japanese Americans were found to be closer to the hypothesized Japanese values than to the Caucasians on each of the measures listed above.

The influence of cultural persistence can be found in Kitano's data (1976:206-207). Kitano states that although with each succeeding generation the trend is toward acculturation, the evidence supports "a high degree of conformity, obedience, a manifestation of ethical behavior, and respect for authority, and a corresponding low degree of acting out, overt rebellion, and independence" (p. 36).

Dependency vs. Independence

Doi (1962) claims that the concept of *amae* (to depend and presume upon another's benevolence) is essential to understanding the personality structure of the Japanese. Dependence on parents is fostered and even institutionalized into its social structure. Physical and psychological dependence between mother and child is found to be well established among the Japanese by the time the infant is three to four months of age (Caudill and Weinstein, 1974). The basic alignment between the mother and child versus the father is noted by Vogel (1963:211) as a division not based on hostility but on psychological and behavioral division within the family. Caudill's study (1950:313-314) indicates dependence on parents persists among the Japanese Americans and that ". . . for Issei and Nisei alike, one never really breaks away from the mother as she continues to remain solidly internalized in the superego throughout life."

One practice that reinforces mutual dependency between parent and child is sleeping arrangements. Caudill and Plath (1974) found that an individual in urban Japan can expect to co-sleep in a two-generation group for more than half of one's life, first as a child and then as a parent. Bathing and eating together are other forms of familial activities which foster mutual dependency in a Japanese family.

Kitano and Kikumura (1976) found that co-sleeping arrangements no longer seem to be the practice among Japanese Americans, although many Nisei recall sleeping first with their parents and then with other siblings. Whether this practice was carried over from Japan because of poverty and the lack of sleeping space or because of preference was not ascertained. But most will agree to the great comfort and security they derived from such an arrangement. Bathing together in a Japanese style *o-furo* (bath) is another family activity that many Nisei recall from their early years, although this activity is no longer practiced among the younger generations.

The differing emphasis on dependency versus independence in American and Japanese cultures has been a source of conflict for many Japanese American families. The push for greater freedom of personal choice and expression of individuality by the Nisei was often challenged by the Issei with increased efforts to retain parental authority. DeVos (1951:270) feels that "the conflicts in the Nisei seem to be concerned with the problem of achieving greater self differentiation rather than accepting the personal submergence emphasized by the other Japanese ideal and the necessity thereby of assuming more rigid and constrictive controls."

Enryo

Enryo [reserve, constraint] helps to explain much of the differences in styles of communication and behavior. As Kitano (1976) indicates, this concept originally referred to the deferential manner in which inferiors were supposed to behave toward their superiors but it was adapted by the Japanese in America to apply to their behavior toward white persons. One of the main manifestations of *enryo* was the conscious use of silence as a safe or neutral response to an embarrassing or ambiguous situation.

The manifestations of *enryo* in Japanese American social interactions are further illustrated by Kitano:

> For example, take observations of Japanese in situations as diverse as their hesitancy to speak out at meetings; their refusal of any invitation, especially the first time; their refusal of a second helping; their acceptance of a less desired object when given a free choice; their lack of verbal participation, especially in an integrated group; their refusal to ask questions; and their hesitancy in asking for a raise in salary — these may all be based on *enryo*. (1976:124–125)

The interaction rules related to the norm of *enryo* are learned early in the Japanese family. A child quickly learns the importance of reticence, modesty, indirection, and humility and is punished for boastful, aggressive, loud, and self-centered behavior. The Japanese child is taught to be sensitive to the reactions of others; therefore in the ideal social interaction with one's peers, neither person dominates the other. To be boastful of one's achievements and to dwell too long on one's own activities or interests is considered bad taste. By bad mouthing one's self and complimenting others, modesty is preserved and self-validation is achieved by both partners.

Wagatsuma (in press) states: "If one speaks without reserve in a given circle or helps themselves uninvited to a person's material possessions, one may be blamed for having no *enryo*. Without *enryo*, one imposes too much of one's need and demands upon others." The social interactional rules related to the norm of *enryo* are not now as explicitly defined as with the preceding generations but one can still observe this pattern in a Japanese American social setting. The following scene, setting, and conversation will help illustrate this point and may proceed somewhat like the following:

> Three Sansei couples gather for a Saturday evening out. The couples, still undecided as to where they should go, gradually feel each other out as to what the others would like to do, making sure that one's individual interest does not dominate over the group.
>
> COUPLE A: Well, where would you like to go tonight?
>
> COUPLE B: Oh, I don't care . . . what are you in the mood for?
>
> COUPLE A: Well, it really doesn't matter to us.
>
> COUPLE B *(anxious to see a movie that they have been waiting to see for months):* I hear there's a good movie playing at Monica I. But it really doesn't matter what we do. What do you guys feel like doing?
>
> COUPLE C: A movie doesn't sound like such a bad idea.
>
> COUPLE A *(having just seen a boring movie last night after which they swore they wouldn't see another movie for at least a month):* It's up to how everyone else feels. We don't care . . .

The conversation continues until everyone has reached a consensus with no party dominating over any other nor directly expressing their individual desires before feeling out the others'. Verbal assertion of one's genuine feelings is often sacrificed for the sake of harmonious interpersonal relationships and group solidarity.

Utilizing the concept of *enryo,* Johnson and Johnson (1975) illustrated how the differences in interaction rules between Japanese Americans and *haoles* [Caucasians] in Hawaii can be the basis for potential difficulties in establishing close interpersonal relationships. Verbal behavior differed markedly between the Japanese and the *haole* in the initial interaction process. The Japanese tended to exhibit quiet agreeableness, awareness of status of the other person, and formality; the *haole* displayed greeting behavior typified by informality, casualness, heartiness, disclosure of personal data, and egalitarianism. While the Japanese may evaluate the *haoles'* heartiness as insincerity and his quick disclosure of personal data as boastfulness, the *haole* may interpret the Japanese's formality, quiet agreeableness, and respect for status as being distant, unemotional, and inscrutable. These differences of style often operated against establishing mutuality and were the basis of much misunderstanding.

Marriage and Parental Authority

The Issei's ability to *gaman* (stick things out at all cost) and their sense of duty and obligation to husband, wife, and children were the bonds that kept the marriages together instead of love and romance. Marriages were arranged by go-betweens; the single aim of the marriage arrangement was to ensure the continuation of the family line. The Issei's effort to maintain the arranged marriage patterns and their adherence to the strict sexual codes based on the samurai ideals intensified the conflict in the parent-child relationship (Iga, 1957). But as open rebellion against arranged marriages and the push for more personal freedom threatened to break the family's foundation, the Issei slowly backed down on their traditional demands.

Failure to live up to parental expectations was a source of strain and conflict for both the Issei and Nisei (Caudill, 1952). For the Nisei, the conflict involved a pull between a strong sense of obligation to their parents, on the one hand, but also a need to integrate into the mainstream of American middle-class life, on the other hand. For the Issei, conflict resided in the vast discrepancies between the ideal family structure that they had emphasized and idealized and the expectations that they held therein, and the actual family structure which was to evolve in their new environment. Added to this was the buried guilt they had about their own failure to meet parental expectations surrounding their family duties and obligations (DeVos, 1974).

Spiro's survey (1955) of literature on the acculturation of American ethnic groups acknowledges that parental authority is seriously diminished as the immigrant family is slowly integrated into the social system of the larger community, forcing the parents to relinquish some aspects of their former educational, economic, and recreational roles. Efforts to retain former authority result in parent-child conflict.

The Issei parents' pressure to pattern their daughters after the overtly submissive Japanese female created another source of conflict and dissatisfaction for the Nisei female. Caudill (1952) discovered that among the Nisei women great hostility and competition were directed toward the Nisei male. Parental expectations involving "proper" female roles seem to continue in the Sansei generation as well. Meredith (1965) observed that among Sansei females great conflict exists in balancing tradition-directed parental expectations and present-directed personal choices.

Recent studies on interracial marriages show outgroup rates approaching a 50 percent level (Kikumura and Kitano, 1973; Omatsu, 1972; Tinker, 1973). Japanese American females continue to dominate the intermarriage statistics as they have in the past, although the gap appears to be closing. An important factor contributing to the historical preponderance of female intermarriage rates is personal dissatisfaction and conflict. Barnett's (1941) case studies of Northwestern California Indians established that personal conflict and dissatisfaction played a critical role in cultural change. He saw the acceptance of new patterns and standards as a means of relieving personal conflict and dissatisfaction. This was found to be the case among many Japanese American females who married out of their group in Los Angeles County (Kikumura, 1975). Personal dissatisfaction among Japanese American women in their expected female roles may also be the primary reason for the observation made by scholars that the females of this group appear to be acculturating more rapidly than the males (Arkoff, Meredith, and

Iwahara, 1962; Caudill, 1952; DeVos, 1951; Fisher and Cleveland, 1958).

Although the high rate of outmarriage among the Japanese Americans can attest to their greater interaction with the majority group, there is evidence that it is still accompanied with a degree of skepticism and anxiety (Kikumura, 1975). The fear of not being accepted by both spouse's families was often expressed by those who married out. The comfort, rapport, security that one Japanese American gets from another was something missed and longed for by many, and the feeling of guilt — of deserting "one's own kind" or of having done something deviant — was felt by others.

CONCLUSION

The root of the Japanese family stems from Tokugawa (1608–1868) and Meiji (1868–1912) Japan, when ideal behavioral standards were patterned after Confucian ethical values that stressed male dominance and clear role prescriptions for each member of the family. Individualism was submerged in favor of a group orientation and values such as duty and obligation were given precedence over preference and voluntarism.

Exposure to the American system resulted in structural changes in the Japanese American family and in modification of the traditional Japanese value system. Nevertheless, family solidarity and retention of certain Japanese values still persist, such as reciprocity, obligation to parents, and interdependence. The Japanese culture, in combination with their lack of power and their high visibility in a race-conscious society, have acted as brakes on total acculturation and assimilation.

By the start of the 1980s there has been a wide diversity among Japanese Americans. Wide-scale intermarriage has taken place so that the variable of physical identifiability, probably the single most important factor in maintaining a Japanese identity, may also be affected. Nevertheless, if past experience can be taken as a guide, the Japanese American family will retain a style that will continue as a combination and/or modification of Japanese and American cultures.

Methodology

One of my personal goals, as an anthropologist and a Japanese American, has been to promote a greater understanding of Asians in America through my research and writing. The area of inquiry that has always intrigued me has involved cultural continuity and change among the Japanese Americans.

The most common approach to past studies done on Japanese Americans and culture change has been based on cross-sectional analysis, whereby the range of variation in behavior, attitudes, and values existing in a society at one point in time is used to infer the process of change. However, some basic weaknesses to this approach obscure the processes of change. First, one loses insight into the motivational processes of the individual and the various circumstances that led to current conditions. The relationship and interplay between the individual and the group, the belief and the norm, are seen only at one moment in time rather than in the total life trajectory of an individual. Second, culture change is portrayed within the context of abstract statistics and generalizations that lack the humanistic quality of life experiences and that obscure the relationship of the individual to the culture and the society. As Kluckhohn comments:

One of the most astonishing gaps in anthropological knowledge is the lack of other than the most general of generalizations as to the regularities in culture change. This, one may suspect, is largely due to the circumstance that anthropologists have thus far viewed these phenomena in too gross a perspective, with too little attention to the concrete individuals in whom changes actually begin. (1945:136)

Allport (1927:56) concurs that, "Acquaintance with particulars is the beginning of knowledge — scientific or otherwise."

In light of these shortcomings in past studies, it was my decision to use the life history approach to investigate the continuity and change in the Japanese American culture by focusing on the life of an Issei woman — my mother. Many questions lingered concerning my mother's past and the Issei woman's experience in general: What were their lives like before coming to America? What were their life experiences after leaving their homeland? What strains and conflicts did they face? What adaptive mechanisms did they use to cope with situations arising in their everyday lives? What specific factors were involved that allowed them to retain the the Japanese culture to a considerable degree and to remain minimally acculturated? The purpose of this study was to gain deeper insight into these questions, using an approach that would capture and portray the life experience of the Issei in a more humanistic fashion than past studies had achieved.

The life history method has been used by anthropologists since the beginnings of the discipline, emerging out of research on Native Americans. It is the most intensive form of interviewing used in fieldwork. Dollard (1953:3) defines life history as "an account of how a new person is added to the group and becomes an adult capable of meeting the traditional expectations of his society for a person of his sex and age . . . it may well be argued that without the life history the transmission of culture forms from one generation to the next cannot be adequately defined."

The professional interest in the individual and the use of life history materials was stimulated by the influence of Paul Radin (1926) and Edward Sapir (1921) since the 1920s and reached its peak several decades later with Du Bois's *The People of Alor* (1944), and Kardiner's *The Psychological Frontiers of Society* (1945). Langness and Frank's review and analysis (1981) of the anthropological approach to life histories indicates a rapidly increasing growth and interest in personal documents as a source of information among professionals in various disciplines.

THE INSIDER-OUTSIDER PERSPECTIVE

A large variety of inquiries have been made about the advantages and limitations of the "outsider" and "insider" perspectives among sociological and anthropological fieldworkers (Golde, 1970; Jones, 1970; Merton, 1972; Nash, 1963; Yang, 1972). It is my belief, contemplating the methodology and the purpose of this investigation, that this study could not have been effectively carried out by an outsider.

On the one hand, advocates for the outsider perspective generally argue that access to authentic knowledge is more obtainable because of the objectivity and scientific detachment with which one can approach one's investigation as a nonmember of the group. On the other hand, proponents of the insider perspective claim that group membership provides special insight into matters (otherwise obscure to others) based on one's knowledge of the language and one's intuitive sensitivity and empathy and understanding of the culture and its people.

Both perspectives confront the researcher with a different set of problems. For example, Delmos Jones (1972) contrasts the advantages for and the limitations on data collection experienced while doing research as an outsider among the Lalu in Northern Thailand and as an insider among blacks in Denver, Colorado. He found that reaching an understanding of the subtleties of communication and mannerisms, which he intuitively knew as an insider among the blacks in Denver, took a considerable amount of time to achieve as an outsider among the Lalu in Thailand. However, possessing an intimate knowledge and understanding of the people and their culture as an insider also limited access to certain types of information. Jones discovered, with the help of students who were mostly white, that some of the women in the rural South craved a particular kind of dirt during pregnancy — knowledge about which he was previously unaware and possibly did not uncover because of the assumption by the informants that he already knew about such health practices.

The different points of view from which the research is conducted will undoubtedly affect the kinds of information collected and the interpretation of the data. However, I agree with Merton's (1972:36) proposal that "We no longer ask whether it is the Insider or the Outsider who has monopolistic or privileged access to social truth; instead, we begin to consider their distinctive and interactive roles in the process of truth seeking." Since both perspectives have the possibility of distortions and preconceptions of social reality, it is the role of the researcher to evaluate the distinctive advantages and limitations of each perspective in relationship to the problem of investigation before conducting his/her research. Liabilities and assets of each perspective will vary and accrue according to the area of inquiry and the methodology employed.

In many cases, even an insider can be an outsider, depending on the definition used by the participant. According to my mother, an outsider is anyone who is *tanin* — that is, anyone who is not related to the family, whether Japanese or not. After asking her if she would have revealed her life experiences, conflicts and strains to anyone other than myself, she replied, "No! You don't disclose your soul to *tanin* (nonrelatives). Just family is all you can trust." When I asked her why, she answered, *"Haji* [shame]. It's a shame to tell other people your problems." She then proceeded to tell me about the neighbor (a Japanese woman) who reminisced over a cup of tea about her "hard life." My mother said she sat there listening but quietly laughing inside. "Why, her stories of hardships were as difficult as eating breakfast in the morning when you're hungry." In my mother's opinion, one should keep one's innermost thoughts to oneself because (as she did with her neighbor), "People will laugh at you and they won't understand. Most Issei feel the same way I do."

However, my mother was pleased with the possibility that her life history may be read by others. This can be explained by her strong desire to establish a bridge of understanding between the Issei, who often led isolated and lonely lives, and the younger generations, whom she feels have a lot to learn from their past.

Although I am a member of the family, the "objectivity" with which the outsider approaches research was not abandoned. Applying Merton's (1972) social structural conception of insiders and outsiders, I was simultaneously an insider (member of the family) and an outsider (occupant of different status set in relation to my being a life history participant). As Merton states, "In structural terms, we are all, of course, both Insiders and Outsiders, members of some groups and, sometimes derivatively, not of others; occupants of certain statuses which thereby exclude us from occupying other cognate statuses." Therefore, ". . . individuals have not a single status set: a complement of variously interrelated statuses which interact to affect both their behavior and perspectives (1972:22)." The status set that distinctly separates me from my mother is generation. My mother is an Issei (first-generation immigrant, born in Japan) and I am a Nisei (second-generation, child of Issei, born in America). The separation of generations is perhaps even greater when one considers the difference in age: My mother is forty years older than I, and if I were classified into generation by age, I would belong to the Sansei (third) generation.

Studies have shown that generational differences within the same culture could be greater than differences within the same generation in separate cultures. Kitano's study (1963) comparing childrearing attitudes between two generations of Japanese women in the United States and two generations of Japanese women in Japan, revealed that there were greater differences between two generations in the same culture than there were between the same generation across national boundaries. The findings of Barrien, Arkoff, and Iwahara (1967) suggest that the social maturational process among Caucasian Americans, Japanese Americans, and Japanese overshadows cultural differences. The generational differences in behavior and perspectives become even greater when comparing the Japanese immigrants with their American-born generation. Even between the

Japanese American-born generations, distinctions exist so that if one says, "I am Nisei" or "I am Sansei," certain assumptions can be made regarding their behavior and values. Because of this generational difference between my mother and myself, the problem of my investigation was approached with the objectivity of the outsider's perspective, but with the benefits often available only to the insider of gaining relatively easy access to information and establishing greater rapport, trust, and understanding.

The Issei often feel that the younger generations have no time to understand their ways or to listen and learn from their experiences of the past. My mother says, "The Nisei and Sansei live in big houses now, but many of them don't know the hardships that their parents suffered to put them where they are today." The interview sessions with my mother served as an opportunity to bridge the generation gap; through the process of listening to her life experiences, values, and concerns, and understanding the important lessons in life that she had to teach me, I was made an insider to her world of the Issei in America.

DATA COLLECTION

Data collection began on April 11, 1975, and continued on through March 1, 1978. Interviews were conducted at the homes of family members and recorded on cassette tapes. Notes were taken simultaneously to facilitate indexing of each taped interview. Tape-recorded interviews with each family member were used to preserve each individual's life story in his/her own words. This technique was used by Oscar Lewis in his study of a Mexican family (1961) and a Puerto Rican family (1966). Lewis's works successfully confirmed that the approach provided "a cumulative, multifaceted, panoramic view of each individual, of the family as a whole . . ." (1961:xi), capturing for the reader "the full flavor of the speech of the people, the slang, the nuances, the hesitations, the laughter, the tears" (1966:xxii).

Data collected from family members other than my mother were used to support the analysis and interpretation of her life history. The total number of hours spent on interviews with each member was as follows:

A. Japanese American Family
    1. Michiko (mother)   288 hours
    2. Hana (second eldest daughter)   32 hours
    3. Keiko (fifth eldest daughter)   32 hours
    4. Yoko (sixth eldest daughter)   12 hours
    5. Harumi (eighth eldest daughter)   12 hours
    6. Hiromi (ninth eldest daughter)   12 hours

                            Subtotal   388 hours

B. Japanese Family (mother's relatives in Hiroshima)
    1. Umetaro (eldest brother)   20 hours
    2. Itsue (eldest brother's wife)   20 hours
    3. Shōsō (eldest brother's eldest son) 20 hours
    4. Haruko (eldest sister)   20 hours
    5. Takejiro (youngest brother)   20 hours

                            Subtotal   100 hours

                                Total   488 hours

I translated from Japanese into English the data collected from my mother and from her family in Hiroshima. When there were doubts as to the accuracy of the translation, Dr. Hiroshi Wagatsuma, Professor at the University of Tsukuba and Visiting Professor in the Department of Anthropology, University of California at Los Angeles, or members of the family were consulted.

PROBLEMS IN METHODOLOGY

Several factors affected my data during the process of collection. First, the fact that I am a participant in the life history affected the data more than any other factor because of my involvement with each of the family members. The very intimate, mutual involvement of researcher to participant and of participants to each other meant that there was a great amount of reactivity affecting each other's lives which often changed the course of the life histories. The reciprocal reactivity of researcher to participant and participant to researcher was dramatically exemplified by an event which changed the course of one of the participant's lives:

In the summer of 1977, I flew to Sacramento to collect data from my sister, Keiko (fifth eldest daughter). I was excited because this was actually the first time in my life that I was to engage in an adult conversation with my older sister. Ten years separated us; the last time we lived together before she got married she was nineteen and I was nine. But as we sat in her kitchen the day I arrived, she expressed the same thoughts that were running through my mind. "Isn't it strange, there are ten years difference between us, but we could relate on the same level." I had finally become her peer.

As our conversation progressed, I suggested that she move into my apartment in Los Angeles. The suggestion was based on a matter of convenience for both of us. She was involved in a relationship from which she wanted escape, and I was planning to move to another state and didn't want to go through the expense or the inconvenience of either moving my furniture or storing it until I returned.

Before the day ended, she had talked herself into moving to Los Angeles. She telephoned her friend, who knew of someone that wanted to rent her house, and she called another contact who could help her find a job in Los Angeles. The full consequences of her move did not dawn on us until we both retired to our separate rooms in the evening.

The next morning we both woke up early. Keiko had spent a sleepless night and she looked haggard. After pouring herself some coffee, she firmly told me, "I changed my mind. I can't move." The rest of the day she spent reaffirming her decision.

I stayed a week with Keiko and stopped in Liberty to interview my sister Hana (second eldest daughter) before heading home. Several days later Keiko called to tell me, "I'll be flying in tomorrow. I have several job interviews lined up." The job interviews were successful and she received five offers before boarding the plane to return the same day that she arrived. She accepted the job with the highest pay and fewest hours and decided to move in a month after finalizing the sale of her house and training a new replacement for her old job.

Keiko sent her daughter to live with me that month, since school started sooner than she could move. Monday, four days before she was to move I was having dinner with one of my sisters and our friends when the phone rang. It was Keiko. "The doctor has found a lump in my breast which is changing shape and I'm going into the hospital tomorrow to have a biopsy taken. I can't move to Los Angeles. If it's cancer I have to stay in Sacramento. I just can't move now." I could detect the urgency in her voice but as she continued, the thought crossed my mind that she really didn't want to move but after finding a new job, selling the house, then sending her daughter to live with me, she needed some drastic excuse to change her mind and save face.

The lump in her breast was cancerous and the evening of her operation I flew up to Sacramento to be with her. When I stepped into her house the walls were bare, everything was packed neatly into labeled boxes, but in the kitchen scattered boxes lay around the cupboards. Her friends had already started to help her unpack that morning after they discovered she had cancer and would no longer be moving to Los Angeles. Everything was to be put back the way it was before. The buyers had agreed to retract the sale and the house was hers again.

Only after returning home and receiving a letter from Keiko, did I realize the full impact that I had on changing her life. It read:

Dear Akemi,

My dear little sister, I have put you through hell and then some! I hope some day that I could repay all that love and compassion to you — but not under the same circumstances of course. You have been very brave and have given me the strength and courage to go on. I feel that I owe my life to you. If you had not talked to me about going to L.A., I probably had only two more years to live. I cannot help but feel that our karma was intertwined since who would ever believe that after all these years apart, your casual suggestion should have made such an impact upon my very existence!

I am feeling better and better every day — may I never forget how grateful I should always be to all of you.

Love,

Keiko

Before moving to Los Angeles, Keiko had decided to get a thorough physical check-up from her family doctor, at which time he discovered the lump in her breast. According to Keiko, she would have waited at least another six months before getting a physical if it were not for the fact that she was moving.

The reactivity of researcher to participant and of participant to researcher is present in all life history taking processes but perhaps more magnified in cases where the researcher is intimately involved in the participant's life. Because of this problem in methodology, I began to record not only the events of the interview situation itself and the specific, present-day events in the participant's life, but also my feelings, reactions, and events in my life which would have direct bearing on the life of my family.

The second factor that affected the data surrounded the creation of a family life history by all the members combined. Events often became so much intermeshed with accounts told by others that one no longer could remember whether she herself had actually experienced the event, or felt she remembered because it had been retold time and again by other family members. I have witnessed this process in family group discussions where one sister would start to talk about an event in the past, then another sister would add on to the account, or another would contradict all that had been said and tell the "true" story, until after awhile the experience had developed into something much larger than it had been before. Often each member would contribute her perception of the story which would spark the memory of another event and in this way, the discussions would touch upon many past events with the assistance of each member's combined memory.

Pressure applied by family members to form congruent family images that are held by the majority affects the life history data that are collected. For example, the majority may hold the image of the mother as a strong and loving person while a few view her as weak and dependent. The few that hold the latter image of their mother are often forced, through family pressure, to conform their views to the majority's. One of the functions that congruent family images help to serve is to promote greater family unity.

Third, the life history participant often assumes that the inside researcher already knows the information since he/she has experienced the same or similar events. This problem was magnified in my study since I am a member of the family. For that reason, I had decided to stop the life history narrative approximately 20 years before the actual time of data collection. Events after that time were often recalled with an economy of detail because my mother assumed that I was old enough to recall them, in some cases more clearly than she.

Fourth, life history data were selectively recalled according to present life situations. The recollection of past events inevitably led to the problems that faced the participant in the present, and those past events were discussed in terms of causes for the participant's present situation. An example of this selectivity process could be observed with Keiko, who chose to recall her past in relation to primarily two topics: the problems she was experiencing in a present relationship and the reasons for her recent divorce. If I would ask her questions about the past, she would eventually gear the discussion back to reasons for the failure of her past marriage or the fulfillments and disappointments in her present relationship. She would analyze her past, searching for reasons that would justify or account for her present situation, and after several hours of talking, she would say, "Listen, I don't want to talk about the past. What's important is what's happening to me right now!"

Fifth, I have found that the kind of data collected from the participant is strongly affected by the events that occur just prior to the interview. An example of the data selection process involved my mother, whom I interviewed immediately after she had a disturbing conversation with her son. She told him that she had decided not to go live in the little house in back of his own which he had recently purchased with the intent of having her live with him. She questioned her son's sincerity, wondering why he was not more persuasive and persistent.

The data I collected that day centered around her disappointment with men in general but with her husband and son in particular. She lectured to me, telling me that a woman must learn how to do things for herself and not to depend on a man; that her entire life was dedicated to her husband and children; and urged me to look at the meager benefits she received for her total dedication. But as the weeks passed she began to accept her decision of not living with her son as one reached through her own volition, and her advice to me had changed. Her disappointment with men still remained, but her views on the woman's role in life differed. She said, "For a woman, the main thing is to take care of her husband and to raise the children. This is where a woman finds her fulfillment. No matter how independent she may be, she must depend on her man because he is the main breadwinner."

I have often heard my mother reiterate this belief to all her daughters. I had never heard her speak differently about a woman's role in life. I knew the disappointment she felt with men in her life, but never before was I more aware of its depths than on that day when she vocalized her anger to me.

Finally, the single largest problem that confronted me was: How would the life history materials that I present affect the family? Although I have the consent to include data given to me from the family members, how would the information affect the others who were directly or indirectly involved in the given events? Issues concerning ethical questions were handled in the following way: First, the names of people and geographic locations were changed; all other data remained factual. Second, all participants were clearly told, before the research, the purpose of the study and the desired end product. Third, all participants were given a copy of the manuscript after its completion, and consulted before publication.

MY ROLE AND RELATIONSHIP TO THE LIFE HISTORY PARTICIPANTS

Since I started collecting life histories, the family has been drawn closer together, creating a greater interdependence among the members for emotional support. My trip to Japan to see our relatives created much excitement. A letter that I had written home to one of my sisters was copied and sent to all the family members. Upon my return from the trip the family gathered to hear the stories and to see the pictures and slides.

My role as the youngest in the family has been beneficial for data collection. I am viewed by my older sisters as a neutral force in the family, since they were married and out of the household by the time I was an adolescent. Experiences shared with each other which would have inhibited discussion of past events and/or present feelings, such as personal grudges or sibling rivalry, were nonexistent, to my knowledge.

As for my mother, each interview session was anxiously awaited and seen as an opportunity to be together and to relate to her youngest daughter the important lessons in life — knowledge that she felt would lead me on to the "right path in life." Data collection was therefore selectively recalled with those thoughts in mind.

Bibliography

Allport, G. 1942. *The Use of Personal Documents in Psychological Science.* SSRC Bulletin 49, New York, pp. xix–210.

Arkoff, A., G. Meredith, and S. Iwahara. 1962. "Dominance-Deferance Patterning in Motherland-Japanese, Japanese-American, and Caucasian-American Students." *Journal of Social Psychology* 58:61–66.

Barnett, H. G. 1941–1942. "Personal Conflicts and Cultural Change." *Social Forces* 20(October-May):160–171.

Befu, H. 1974. "Gift-Giving in a Modernizing Japan." In Takie Sugiyama Lebra and William P. Lebra, *Japanese Culture and Behavior.* Honolulu: University Press of Hawaii.

Benedict, R. 1948. "Continuities and Discontinuities in Cultural Conditioning." In Clyde Kluckhohn and Henry A. Murray, eds., *Personality in Nature, Society, and Culture.* New York: Alfred A. Knopf, pp. 414–423.

Benedict, R. 1946. *The Chrysanthemum and the Sword.* Boston: Houghton Mifflin.

Berrien, F. K., A. Arkoff, and S. Iwahara. 1967. "Generational Differences in Values: Americans, Japanese Americans, and Japanese." *Journal of Social Psychology* 71:169–175.

Broom, L., and J. Kitsuse. 1955. "The Validation of Acculturation: A Condition to Ethnic Assimilation." *American Anthropologist* 57 (February): 44–48.

Burgess, E. W., and J. J. Locke. 1953. *The Family*. New York: American Book Co.

Caudill, W. 1952. "Japanese American Personality and Acculturation." *Genetic Psychology Monographs* 45(1):3–102.

Caudill, W., and L. Frost. 1974. "A Comparison of Maternal Care and Infant Behavior in Japanese-American, American, and Japanese Families." In William P. Lebra, ed., *Youth, Socialization, and Mental Health*. Honolulu: University Press of Hawaii.

Caudill, W., and D. W. Plath. 1974. "Who Sleeps by Whom? Parent-Child Involvement in Urban Japanese Families." In Takie Sugiyama Lebra and William P. Lebra, eds., *Japanese Culture and Behavior*. Honolulu: University Press of Hawaii, pp. 277–312.

Caudill W., and C. Schooler. 1973. "Child Behavior and Child Rearing in Japan and the United States: An Interim Report." *Journal of Nervous and Mental Disease* 157(5):323–338.

Caudill, W., and H. Weinstein. 1974. "Maternal Care and Infant Behavior in Japan and America." In Takie Sugiyama Lebra and William P. Lebra, eds., *Japanese Culture and Behavior*. Honolulu: University Press of Hawaii, pp. 225–276.

Connor, J. W. 1974a. "Acculturation and Changing Need Patterns in Japanese-American and Caucasian-American College Students." *Journal of Social Psychology* 93:293–294.

Connor, J. W. 1974b. "Acculturation and Family Continuities in Three Generations of Japanese Americans." *Journal of Marriage and the Family* 36(February): 159–165.

Connor, J. W. 1974c. "Value Continuities and Change in Three Generations of Japanese Americans." *Ethos* 2(3):232-264.

Daniels, R. 1972. *Concentration Camps U.S.A.* New York: Holt.

Daniels, R., and H. H. L. Kitano. 1970. *American Racism: Exploration of the Nature of Prejudice.* Englewood Cliffs, N.J.: Prentice-Hall.

DeVos, G. 1951. *Acculturation and Personality Structure: A Rorschach Study of Japanese Americans.* Ph.D. Dissertation for the University of Chicago, Chicago, Illinois.

DeVos, G. 1974. "The Relation of Guilt toward Parents to Achievement and Arranged Marriage among the Japanese." In Takie Sugiyama Lebra and William P. Lebra, eds., *Japanese Culture and Behavior.* Honolulu: University Press of Hawaii.

DeVos G., and H. Wagatsuma. 1961. "Value Attitudes toward Role Behavior of Women in Two Japanese Villages." *American Anthropologist* 63(2):1204-1230.

DeVos, G., and H. Wagatsuma. 1966. *Japan's Invisible Race.* Berkeley: University of California Press.

Doi, T. L. 1962. "Amae: A Key Concept for Understanding Japanese Personality Structure," In R. J. Smith and R. K. Beardsley, eds., *Japanese Culture: Its Development and Characteristics.* Chicago: Aldine Publishing Co.

Dollard, J. 1935. *Criteria for the Life History.* New Haven: Yale University Press.

Dore, R. P. 1958. *City Life in Japan.* Berkeley: University of California Press.

Du Bois, Cora A. 1944. *The People of Alor.* New York: Harper.

Fisher, L. H. "History of Contract Labor in California Agriculture." In *The Harvest Labor Market in California.* Cambridge: 1953: pp. 20-41.

Fisher, S., and S. E. Cleveland. 1958. *Body Image and Personality.* Princeton: D. Van Nostrand.

French, T. M. 1941. "A Goal, Mechanism, and Integrative Field." *Psychosomatic Medicine* 3:226–252. As quoted in William Caudill, 1952.

Gee, E. 1971. "Issei: The First Women." In *Asian Women,* Asian American Studies Center, University of California, Berkeley, pp. 8–15.

Girdner, A., and A. Loftis. 1970. *The Great Betrayal.* London: Macmillan.

Golde, P., ed. 1970. *Women in the Field.* Chicago: Aldine.

Goode, W. J. 1963. *World Revolution and Family.* New York: Free Press of Glencoe.

Ichihashi, Y. 1969. *Japanese in the United States.* New York: Arno Press and the *New York Times.*

Iga, M. 1957. "The Japanese Social Structure and the Source of Mental Strains of Japanese Immigrants in the United States." *Social Forces* 35:271–278.

Ito, K. 1973. *Issei: A History of Japanese Immigrants in North America.* Seattle. Pp. 247–288. (Published by the Executive Committee for the Publication of *Issei,* etc. Current address: c/o Japanese Community Service, 1414 S. Weller St., Seattle, WA 98144.)

Johnson, C. L. 1977. "Interdependence, Reciprocity and Indebtedness: An Analysis of Japanese American Kinship Relations." *Journal of Marriage and the Family* 1977, 39(May):351–363.

Johnson, C. L., and F. A. Johnson. 1975. "Interaction Rules and Ethnicity: The Japanese and Caucasians in Honolulu." *Social Forces* 52(2):452–456.

Jones, D. J. 1970. "Towards a Native Anthropology." *Human Organization* 29(4) (Winter):251–259.

Kardiner, A. (with the collaboration of Ralph Linton, Cora Du Bois, and James West). 1945. *The Psychological Frontiers of Society.* New York: Columbia University Press.

Kikumura, A. 1975. "Japanese American Outmarriages in Los Angeles County 1971–1972." Unpublished Master's Thesis for the Department of Anthropology at University of California, Los Angeles.

Kikumura, A., and H. H. L. Kitano. 1973. "Interracial Marriage: A Picture of the Japanese Americans." *Journal of Social Issues* 29(2):67–81.

Kitano, H. H. L. 1963. "Inter- and Intragenerational Differences in Maternal Attitudes towards Child-rearing." *Journal of Social Psychology* 63:215–220.

Kitano, H. H. L. 1976. *Japanese Americans: The Evolution of a Subculture.* Englewood Cliffs, N.J.: Prentice-Hall.

Kitano, H. H. L., and A. Kikumura. 1976. "The Japanese Family Life Style." In Charles Mindel and Robert Habenstein, eds., *Ethnic Families in America.* New York: Elsevier Press, pp. 41–60.

Kluckhohn, C. 1945. *The Personal Document in Anthropological Science.* In *The Use of Personal Documents in History, Anthropology and Sociology.* SSRC Bulletin, 53.

Langness, L. L., and G. Frank. 1981. *Lives: An Anthropological Approach to Biography.* Novato, California: Chandler and Sharp.

Lebra, T. S. 1974. "Reciprocity and the Asymmetric Principle: An Analytical Reappraisal of the Japanese Concept of *On.*" In Takie Sugiyama Lebra and William P. Lebra, eds., *Japanese Culture and Behavior.* Honolulu: University Press of Hawaii, pp. 192–209.

Levine, G. N., and D. M. Montero. 1973. "Socioeconomic Mobility among Three Generations of Japanese Americans." *Journal of Social Issues* 29(2):33–48.

Levy, M. J. 1975. "Aspects of the Analysis of Family Structure." In A. J. Coale, L. A. Fallers, M. J. Levy Jr., D. M. Schneider, and S. S. Tomkins, *Aspects of the Analysis of Family Structure.* Princeton, N.J.: Princeton University Press.

Lewis, O. 1961. *The Children of Sanchez.* New York: Vintage Books.

Lewis, O. 1968. *La Vida*. New York: Random House.

Meredith, G. M. 1965. "Observations on the Acculturation of Sansei Japanese Americans in Hawaii." *Psychologia* 8(1-2)(June):41-49.

Merton, R. K. 1972. "Insiders and Outsiders: A Chapter in the Sociology of Knowledge." *American Journal of Sociology* 78(1)(July):9-47.

Nash, D. 1963. "The Ethnologist as Stranger: An Essay in the Sociology of Knowledge." *Southwestern Journal of Anthropology* 19:149-167.

Omatsu, G. 1972. "Nihonmachi Beat." *Hokubei Mainichi*. January 12, 1972.

Parsons, T. 1954. "Democracy and Social Structure in Pre-Nazi Germany," In *Essays in Sociological Theory*. Glencoe, Illinois: Free Press.

Petersen, W., 1971. *Japanese Americans*. New York: Random House.

Radin, P., ed. 1926. *Crashing Thunder: The Autobiography of an American Indian*. New York: D. Appleton.

Raushenbush, W., 1926. "Their Place in the Sun." *Survey Graphic* 16(May):154-159. As quoted by Stanford Lyman in *The Asian in North America*. Santa Barbara, California: American Bibliographical Center, Clio Press.

Redfield, R., R. Linton, and M. M. Herskovits. 1936. "A Memorandum for the Study of Acculturation." *American Anthropologist* 38:149-152.

Ruesch, J. 1948. "Social Techniques, Social Status, and Social Change in Illness." In C. Kluckhohn and H. A. Murray, eds., *Personality in Nature, Society, and Culture*. New York: Alfred A. Knopf.

Sapir, E., "The Life of a Nootka Indian." *Queens Quarterly* 28:232-243. Reprinted in Elsie Clews Parsons, ed., *American Indian Life*. New York: B. W. Huebsch.

Spindler, L., and G. Spindler. 1958. "Male and Female Adaptation in Cultural Change." *American Anthropologist* 60:217-233.

Spiro, M. E. 1955. "The Acculturation of American Ethnic Groups," *American Anthropologist* 57:1240–1252.

TenBroek, J., E. N. Barnhart, and F. W. Matson. 1968. *Prejudice, War and the Constitution.* Berkeley and Los Angeles: University of California Press.

Teske, R. H. C., and B. H. Nelson. 1973. "Acculturation and Assimilation: A Clarification." *American Ethnologist* 2(May):351–367.

Tinker, J. N. 1973. "Intermarriage and Ethnic Boundaries: The Japanese American Case." *Journal of Social Issues* 29(2)49–66.

Vogel, E. F. 1963. *Japan's New Middle Class.* Berkeley and Los Angeles: University of California Press.

Wagatsuma, H. 1977. "Some Aspects of the Contemporary Japanese Family: Once Confucian, Now Fatherless?" *Daedalus* 106(2): 181–210.

Wagatsuma, H. In Press. "Entries for Encyclopedia of Japan." Kodansha International.

Wagatsuma, H., and G. DeVos. 1962. "Attitudes toward Arranged Marriage in Rural Japan." *Human Organization* 21:187–200.

Warner, W. L., and L. Srole. 1945. *The Social Systems of American Ethnic Groups.* New Haven: Yale University Press.

Yanagisako, S. J. 1975. "Two Processes of Change in Japanese-American Kinship." *Journal of Anthropological Research* 31(3)Autumn: 196–224

Yanagisako, S. J. 1977. "Women-centered Kin Networks in Urban Bilateral Kinship." *American Ethnologist* 4(2):207–226.

Yang, M. C. 1972. "How *A Chinese Village* Was Written." In Solon T. Kimball and James B. Watson, eds., *Crossing Cultural Boundaries: The Anthropological Experience.* San Francisco: Chandler Publishing Co., pp. 63–73.